Charles Dwight Sigsbee

The Maine

An Account of her Destruction in Havana Harbor

Charles Dwight Sigsbee

The Maine
An Account of her Destruction in Havana Harbor

ISBN/EAN: 9783744714686

Printed in Europe, USA, Canada, Australia, Japan

Cover: Foto ©ninafisch / pixelio.de

More available books at **www.hansebooks.com**

CAPTAIN CHARLES DWIGHT SIGSBEE, U. S. N.

The "Maine"
An Account of her Destruction in Havana Harbor

THE PERSONAL
NARRATIVE OF

Captain Charles D. Sigsbee
U. S. N.

NEW YORK
THE CENTURY CO.
1899

Copyright, 1898, 1899, by
THE CENTURY CO.

THE DE VINNE PRESS

TO MY SHIPMATES OF THE "MAINE," THE DEAD AND THE LIVING, I DEDICATE THIS, MY PERSONAL NARRATIVE OF THE GREAT DISASTER.

THE AUTHOR.

CONTENTS

		PAGE
I	Our Reception at Havana	1
II	The Explosion	59
III	The Wrecking and the Inquiry	125

APPENDICES

APPENDIX		PAGE
A	Technical Description of the "Maine"	195
B	For the "Vizcaya's" Safety	203
C	Full Findings of the United States Court of Inquiry	207
D	Message of the President of the United States	213
E	Ensign Powelson's Personal Report to Captain Sigsbee on the Cause of the Explosion of the "Maine"	219
F	Finding of the Spanish Court of Instruction [Inquiry]	231
G	Names and Rates of the Members of the "Maine's" Crew	246
H	Burial and Identification List of the "Maine's" Dead	257

LIST OF ILLUSTRATIONS

CAPTAIN CHARLES DWIGHT SIGSBEE, U. S. N. . . *Frontispiece*
From a photograph by Parker, Washington, D. C.

FACING PAGE

THE CREW OF THE "MAINE" RETURNING FROM SHORE-DRILL, AT FORT MONROE 4
From a photograph by E. H. Hart, Brooklyn, N. Y.

GENERAL FITZHUGH LEE, UNITED STATES CONSUL-GENERAL AT HAVANA 8
From a photograph by E. H. Hart, made on the deck of the "Montgomery."

LIEUTENANT-COMMANDER ADOLPH MARIX, FORMER EXECUTIVE OFFICER OF THE "MAINE" 12
From a photograph by E. H. Hart.

CAPTAIN CROWNINSHIELD (DURING THE SPANISH WAR A MEMBER OF THE NAVAL BOARD) RECEIVING MR. HERBERT, THEN SECRETARY OF THE NAVY, ON BOARD THE "MAINE" 16
From a photograph by E. H. Hart.

THE "MAINE" ENTERING HAVANA HARBOR, MORRO CASTLE ON THE RIGHT 20

VIEW OF HAVANA HARBOR FROM A WHARF IN REGLA—I 24
From a photograph by E. H. Hart.

VIEW OF HAVANA HARBOR FROM A WHARF IN REGLA—II 28
From a photograph by E. H. Hart.

List of Illustrations

FACING PAGE

THE "MAINE" SALUTING THE SPANISH FLAG AFTER MAKING FAST TO THE OFFICIAL BUOY, AT WHICH SHE WAS DESTROYED 32

LUNCHEON GIVEN AT THE HAVANA YACHT-CLUB AT 11 A. M., JANUARY 30, 1898, BY UNITED STATES CONSUL-GENERAL FITZHUGH LEE, TO THE CAPTAIN AND OFFICERS OF THE U. S. S. "MAINE" 34
From a photograph by Gomez de la Carretez.

FACSIMILE OF THE CIRCULAR HANDED TO CAPTAIN SIGSBEE ON HIS WAY TO THE BULL-FIGHT AND LATER SENT TO HIM THROUGH THE HAVANA POST-OFFICE . 37

CAPTAIN SIGSBEE, GENERAL FITZHUGH LEE, SEVERAL OFFICERS OF THE "MAINE," AND CIVILIANS AT THE HAVANA YACHT-CLUB 40
From a photograph by Gomez de la Carretez.

CAPTAIN SIGSBEE IN THE CAPTAIN'S CABIN ON BOARD THE "MAINE" 44

THE WARD-ROOM OF THE "MAINE" 48
From a photograph by E. H. Hart.

CAPTAIN-GENERAL RAMON BLANCO 52
From a photograph by E. H. Hart.

SIGNAL-DRILL ON THE DECK OF THE "MAINE" . . . 56
From a photograph by E. H. Hart.

THE MAINTOP 60

THE "MAINE" IN DRY-DOCK NO. 2, NEW YORK NAVY-YARD 61
From a photograph by Enrique Muller.

PRIVATE WILLIAM ANTHONY 64
From a photograph by C. J. Horner, Boston, Mass.

INBOARD PROFILE OF THE "MAINE" 67

CHIEF MACHINISTS' CABIN 68
From a photograph by E. H. Hart.

List of Illustrations

	FACING PAGE
PLANS OF MAIN AND BERTH DECKS	71
THE LAST SCENE ON THE SINKING DECK OF THE "MAINE"	72
MIDSHIP SECTION	73
PLANS OF PROTECTIVE AND SUPERSTRUCTURE DECKS	75
FACSIMILE, REDUCED, OF CAPTAIN SIGSBEE'S MESSAGE TO THE SECRETARY OF THE NAVY, "SECNAV" BEING THE TELEGRAPHIC ADDRESS OF THE LATTER	76
HOLD PLAN AND PLAN OF PLATFORM-DECK	79
FACSIMILE OF THE DESPATCH WRITTEN ON AN ENVELOP, SENT ON THE NIGHT OF THE EXPLOSION	80
VIEW OF THE WRECK FROM THE STERN	84
From a photograph by E. H. Hart.	
THE CENTRAL SUPERSTRUCTURE, INCLUDING THE CONNING-TOWER, THROWN UPSIDE DOWN	88
From a photograph by E. H. Hart.	
THE AFTER TORPEDO-TUBE	92
From a photograph by E. H. Hart.	
LIEUTENANT FRIEND W. JENKINS	96
From a photograph by B. L. H. Dabbs, Pittsburg, Pa.	
ASSISTANT ENGINEER DARWIN R. MERRITT	96
VIEW MADE SEVERAL DAYS AFTER THE EXPLOSION	100
From a photograph by E. H. Hart.	
BOTTOM-PLATING, PROTECTIVE DECK, AND SECOND LONGITUDINAL SHOWING ABOVE THE WATER	104
From a photograph by E. H. Hart.	
FUNERAL OF NINETEEN OF THE "MAINE'S" DEAD, FROM THE MUNICIPAL PALACE, HAVANA	108
From a photograph by E. H. Hart.	
GRAVE OF THE "MAINE'S" DEAD IN THE CEMETERY AT HAVANA	112
From a photograph by E. H. Hart.	

List of Illustrations

FACING PAGE

THE "MAINE'S" BASEBALL NINE AS ORGANIZED AT THE
TIME OF THE EXPLOSION 116
From a photograph by E. H. Hart.

MINSTREL GROUP WHO PERFORMED AT THE ENTERTAINMENT GIVEN BY THE CREW OF THE "MAINE" TO THE
CREW OF THE "COLUMBIA" 120
From a photograph by E. H. Hart.

THE COURT OF INQUIRY ON BOARD THE "MANGROVE" 125
From a photograph by E. H. Hart.

SURVIVORS AT THE HOSPITAL, KEY WEST, MAKING THE
INITIAL OF THE LOST SHIP 127
From a photograph by E. H. Hart.

ENSIGN W. V. N. POWELSON, U. S. N. 128
From a photograph by E. H. Hart.

KEY RECOVERED FROM THE WRECK OF THE "MAINE" 131

HAVANA PASSENGER-BOATS AROUND THE SPANISH
CRUISER "VIZCAYA" ON A VISITING DAY 132
From a photograph by E. H. Hart.

THE "MONTGOMERY" SALUTING AFTER MOORING AT
HAVANA 136
From a photograph by E. H. Hart.

WRECKING WITH THE AID OF HYDRAULIC JACKS . . . 140
From a photograph by E. H. Hart.

EXPERT DIVER ANDREW OLSEN PREPARING TO DESCEND 146
Redrawn from a photograph by E. H. Hart.

GROUP OF PETTY OFFICERS ON BOARD THE "MAINE" . 152
From a photograph by E. H. Hart.

REVOLVER-DRILL ON THE STARBOARD SUPERSTRUCTURE
OF THE "MAINE" 156
From a photograph by E. H. Hart.

SPANISH DIVERS AT WORK OUTSIDE THE WRECK OF THE
"MAINE" 160
From a photograph by E. H. Hart.

List of Illustrations

FACING PAGE

A VIEW OF THE SMOKING WRECK OF THE "MAINE," TAKEN EARLY IN THE MORNING AFTER THE EXPLOSION . . 164
From a photograph by George Bronson Rea.

LIEUTENANT-COMMANDER RICHARD WAINWRIGHT, EXECUTIVE OFFICER OF THE "MAINE" 168
From a photograph by E. H. Hart.

LIEUTENANT JOHN J. BLANDIN 172
From a photograph by R. W. Harrison, Selma, Ala.

NAVAL CADET DAVID F. BOYD, JR. 176
From a photograph by Buffham, Annapolis, Md.

SURGEON LUCIEN G. HENEBERGER 176
From a photograph by Prince, Old Point Comfort, Va.

PAYMASTER CHARLES M. RAY 176
From a photograph by A. Farsari & Co., Yokohama, Japan.

LIEUTENANT ALBERTUS W. CATLIN 176
From a photograph by A. E. Tuck, Gloversville, N. Y.

CARPENTER GEORGE HELMS 176
From a photograph by R. Weiss, Brooklyn, N. Y.

PAY-CLERK BRENT MCCARTHY 176
From a photograph by A. Farsari & Co., Yokohama, Japan.

GUNNER JOSEPH HILL 176
From a photograph by S. Young, New York.

NAVAL CADET ARTHUR CRENSHAW 180
From a photograph by Prince, Old Point Comfort, Va.

PASSED ASSISTANT ENGINEER FREDERIC C. BOWERS . 180
From a photograph by Butler, Brooklyn, N. Y.

BOATSWAIN FRANCIS E. LARKIN 180
From a photograph by F. Gutekunst, Philadelphia, Pa.

CHAPLAIN JOHN P. CHIDWICK 180
From a photograph by Anderson, New York.

CHIEF ENGINEER CHARLES P. HOWELL 180
From a photograph by Pach Bros., New York.

NAVAL CADET POPE WASHINGTON 180
From a photograph by Buffham, Annapolis, Md.

List of Illustrations

	FACING PAGE
ASSISTANT ENGINEER JOHN R. MORRIS	180
From a photograph by Prince, New York and Washington, D. C.	
DIAGRAM SHOWING HOW A MINE MIGHT HAVE BEEN PLACED UNDER THE "MAINE"	182
LIEUTENANT JOHN HOOD	184
LIEUTENANT GEORGE P. BLOW	184
From a photograph by Moore, New Orleans, La.	
NAVAL CADET JONAS H. HOLDEN	184
From a photograph by Hart.	
LIEUTENANT GEORGE F. W. HOLMAN	184
From a photograph by Weiss, New York.	
LIEUTENANT CARL W. JUNGEN	184
From a photograph by Rice, Washington, D. C.	
NAVAL CADET WATT T. CLUVERIUS	184
From a photograph by G. Moses & Son, New Orleans, La.	
NAVAL CADET AMON BRONSON, JR.	184
From a photograph by J. W. Taylor, Rochester, N. Y.	
THE SECOND-CLASS BATTLE-SHIP "MAINE," BLOWN UP IN HAVANA HARBOR, FEBRUARY 15, 1898	188

THE "MAINE"

THE "MAINE"

I

OUR RECEPTION AT HAVANA

THE explosion of the *Maine* at Havana, on February 15, 1898, was the ultimate incident which impelled the people of the United States to regard Spain as an impossible neighbor. Although the war which followed was not founded on the destruction of the *Maine* as a political cause, that disaster was the pivotal event of the conflict which has terminated Spanish possession in the Western World. Considerations like these must continue to give the *Maine* a unique place in the history of the United States, especially since the character and magnitude of the disaster make it one of the most shocking on record.

The story of the *Maine* leading up to the explosion may be said to begin at the Southern

The "Maine"

drill-ground of the North Atlantic Squadron, as far back as October 9, 1897. The *New York, Iowa, Brooklyn, Massachusetts, Indiana, Texas,* and *Maine* — all now historic — had been on a cruise along the New England coast, ending at Bar Harbor on August 31. From Bar Harbor they proceeded in squadron to the Southern drill-ground, about twenty-five miles to the eastward of Cape Charles, a locality set apart for drills by reason of its comparative remoteness from the common commercial route of coasting-vessels, as well as its convenient depth of water for anchorage. The squadron was under the command of Rear-Admiral Montgomery Sicard. The night of October 8 terminated a period of hard work of the kind which brought overwhelming victory later. Part of the time had been spent at Hampton Roads in recoaling, and at Yorktown in sham fighting on shore, and in small-arms target practice. The days at sea had been spent in squadron evolutions, target practice, and signaling, and the nights, at least in part, in night-signaling, search-light drill, and in secondary-battery practice, simulating the conditions of attack by torpedo-boats. It was not mere routine; it was the business of warfare, pursued with stern official conscience, under a commander-in-chief who throughout his whole

Our Reception at Havana

career had been conspicuous for official conscience.

On the night of October 8, the squadron was at the Southern drill-ground awaiting the arrival of the *Brooklyn*, which had gone to Hampton Roads for minor repairs. It was expected that the whole squadron would get under way for Boston that night. We of the *Maine* were wondering at the delay of the *Brooklyn*, when, toward midnight, the torpedo-boats *Dupont* and *Ericsson* joined the squadron from Hampton Roads, with despatches for the commander-in-chief. As a result of these despatches, the *Indiana* (Captain H. C. Taylor) was detached and sent to Hampton Roads, and the *Maine*, my command, to Port Royal, South Carolina. The *Indiana* got away during the night, but the *Maine* was repairing some injury, and did not part company with the squadron until dawn of the following day. Thus began a virtually unbroken tour of independent service for the *Maine*, which was connected more or less intimately with the disturbed condition of affairs in Cuba, and culminated in the explosion at Havana.

The *Maine* arrived in Port Royal Sound on October 12. The next day she was taken up the river, and moored in a hole just large enough to fit her, immediately above the naval station, and about four miles below Beaufort. She remained there until November 15. Having visited the place before, she excited no interest among the people of that locality. Excepting our pleasant association with friends at the naval station, we had a dull time. Having been ordered to Port Royal unexpectedly, the depleted state of my own larder made it difficult for me to return the dinners given me at the station. I resorted to invention, which suggested roast pig highly ornamented. My pig was brought on the table whole, bearing a silken banner emblazoned with the legend: "This little pig went to market." My guests were courteous enough to make me believe that the pig was acceptable. My next subterfuge was to have been a possum. I had him undergoing the fattening process, but the *Maine* left before he had reached an amplitude that was satisfactory. One Sunday morning some of us were taken to a negro church by a party from the station. The officiating clergyman was a stout, thick-set negro, doubtless a very good man. He felt keenly the difficulty of preaching to a well-educated party of white people, and remarked, with some concern, "You got me in a tight place." After the prayer and hymn, he announced his text with a striking attitude. With uplifted hands and wide-

THE CREW OF THE "MAINE" RETURNING FROM SHORE-DRILL, AT FORT MONROE.

spread arms, he paused for attention, and, getting it, gave the text, which was: "I am the rose of Sharon, and the lily of the valley." He said various things strange to cultivated ears, but his sermon was effective, and deeply impressed those for whom it was primarily intended.

Although my orders to Port Royal gave me no information as to the purpose, it was hoped at the time that the ship might be able to dock there; but the water outside the dock proved to be too shallow. It is probable, however, that in the visit of the *Maine* to Port Royal it was intended to have a United States man-of-war nearer Cuba. Many citizens were then very restless as to the safety of our own people in that island. I had no instructions to take any measures whatever; the *Maine* was simply awaiting further orders. She made good use of her time at Port Royal. The battalion was repeatedly landed and drilled at the station; every member of the crew was given target practice with small arms, and her ten-inch guns were tested for rapidity of fire. It was the custom in the North Atlantic Squadron to have aiming-drills every afternoon on week-days. No scheme alone can teach gunners to hit. Correct aim comes from practice — and more practice.

The "Maine"

We left Port Royal on November 15, as already stated, and steamed north to the Norfolk navy-yard, where the vessel was docked and put under slight repairs. While at Norfolk, Lieutenant-Commander Adolph Marix, the executive officer,—and a very able one,—was detached. He was succeeded by Lieutenant-Commander Richard Wainwright, who afterward got his opportunity, and distinguished himself in command of the *Gloucester*, off Santiago de Cuba.

The *Maine* and the *Texas* were the first of the modern steel battle-ships built by the United States. The *Maine* was originally designed as an armored cruiser, with a considerable spread of square canvas. Her sail plan in my possession shows her as a bark with squaresails to topgallantsails, but no headbooms. It was then contemplated to give her 7135 square feet of canvas. Later, sails were abandoned, and she was styled a *second-class battle-ship*. She was designed at the Navy Department and built at the New York navy-yard. Her keel was laid October 17, 1888; she was launched November 18, 1890, commissioned September 17, 1895. and left the navy-yard at 10 A. M. on November 5, 1895, drawing 22 feet and 1 inch forward and 21 feet and 8 inches aft. When fully supplied with coal and provisions she was "down by the head." The *Maine* differed greatly in appearance from all other vessels of the United States navy. Instead of one superstructure, as commonly seen, she had three, forward, after, and central. All were of the same breadth transversely. Their sides at the bow and stern were formed by the continuation upward of the outside skin of the ship. Along the sides of the superstructures there was a clear deck-space affording enough room for formations and drills. I have frequently been asked to state the color of the *Maine's* outside paintwork. Her hull was white to the rail; the superstructures, funnels, and masts, and all permanent fittings above the rail except the pilot-house, were dark straw-color. The pilot-house was of varnished mahogany. The boats and bower-anchors were white; the guns and search-lights were black. There were larger ships in the navy than the *Maine*, but none more delightful to command or to serve in. Her quarters were ample for everybody, although certain compartments were rather too hot for comfort in warm weather. The members of the crew were berthed chiefly in the forward and the central superstructures, and on the berth-deck forward of the junior officers' quarters. This distribution of the crew, when considered in connection with the region of the explosion, explains the loss of so many of the crew as compared with the officers. The quarters of the officers were aft; mine were in the after-superstructure, all of which had been apportioned to quarters for a flag-officer and the captain. The *Maine* was not a flagship; therefore the captain acquired the admiral's quarters in addition to his own. The ward-room state-rooms were on the berth-deck, below the captain's cabin. On the starboard side of the compartment immediately forward of the ward-room was the ward-room officers' mess-room; and forward of this, also on the starboard side, and in the same compartment, were the junior officers' quarters. All forward of this compartment was assigned to the crew. It was chiefly on the berth-deck that the greatest destruction of sleeping men resulted from the explosion. The *Maine* had two "winged" or "sponsoned" turrets; that is to say, they were at the sides and projected a few feet beyond the hull. They were placed between the superstructures, one on each side of the ship, as is shown in the many photographs of the vessel. In each were two ten-inch breech-loading rifles. In addition, she carried six six-inch breech-loading rifles, besides seven six-pounder and eight one-pounder rapid-firing rifles. She had four above-water

GENERAL FITZHUGH LEE, UNITED STATES
CONSUL-GENERAL AT HAVANA.

From a photograph made on the deck of
the *Montgomery*.

torpedo-tubes on her berth-deck, all in broadside. The arrangement of her compartments was simple for a battle-ship, so she responded readily to any work done on her to make her look clean and orderly. She had two hundred and fourteen water-tight compartments, as ascertained by a recent inspection of her drawings. All that were not occupied by the officers or crew were closed at night. The following are statistics relating to her: extreme length, 324 feet; beam, 57 feet; displacement, 6650 tons; indicated horse-power, 9290; trial speed, 17.45 knots. She had an armored belt extending 180 feet at the waterline on each side, over which was a flat, armored deck. Joining the two forward ends of the belt was a heavy steel bulkhead, at the bottom of which was an armored deck that continued to the stem. The flat steel deck above armor dipped down abaft the belt, and was continued to the stern, one deck below, with a slightly diminished thickness. Her barbettes and turrets were of heavy steel. The barbettes rested on the armored deck below. A more complete description of the *Maine* is given in Appendix A.

From Norfolk the *Maine* was ordered to Key West, where she arrived on December 15, and moored in the harbor off the city. My orders there were confidential, but they were of such a

The "Maine"

nature that they might at any time have been made public with propriety, had the government so desired. They were, in brief, that the *Maine* was to proceed to Havana in case of grave local disturbances in that city, to give asylum to American citizens, and to afford them the usual protection. The immediate judgment as to the necessity for the services of the *Maine* was to come from General Fitzhugh Lee, United States consul-general at Havana. I promptly opened communication with General Lee, both by letter and by telegraph. My letters were sent in such a way as to be entirely secret. There was no impropriety in the measures that were taken. True or false, the Havana post-office was not free from the suspicion of delaying letters. It was arranged between General Lee and myself that on the receipt from him, by telegraph or otherwise, of the words "Two dollars," the *Maine* was to make preparations to start for Havana two hours after further notice. The actual start was to be made on the receipt of a second preconcerted message.

The form of our correspondence was a matter between General Lee and myself. Toward the last it was deemed necessary to make occasional tests to ascertain if telegraphic communication continued open. Therefore nearly every day I sent a message to General Lee, and he answered

Our Reception at Havana

it. Some of these were rather absurd. In one I inquired of General Lee the state of the weather on the south side of Cuba. He promptly replied that he did not know—which was quite as gratifying as if he had been fully informed. At another time I cabled, "What is the price of bullfight fans?" to which he replied, giving me quotations. Afterward I bought some of the fans commonly used, as souvenirs of a Havana visit, and they were lost with the *Maine*.

One night, about six or seven o'clock, I received the preliminary message. The *Maine* was immediately prepared for sea. Knowing that Key West would be alert as to any sign of movement, I gave orders that all hands should repair on board immediately upon the firing of a gun from the *Maine;* then, in company with a number of the officers, I went on shore to a dance at the hotel, my particular object being to divert suspicion. I was asked a number of questions as to the departure of the *Maine;* but we had managed so well that some of the crew had already given out that we were going to New York.

The final message to the *Maine* from General Lee never came. During the whole visit I was kept fully informed as to the state of affairs at Havana. The riot that occurred in the streets on January 12, in which certain newspaper offices were the chief object of attack, most naturally led us to fear that there might be danger to American citizens.

It is probable that too great importance was attached to that riot by the press of the United States: early news is not always the most accurate news; nevertheless, it was sufficiently grave when viewed by a country which could not control the situation and whose interests were involved. The continued immunity of those who participated seemed to give promise of further trouble. Like most riots, that one was swelled by unexpected numbers—and purposes, too, probably. With excited mobs it is a short and rapid step from one purpose to another: the final purpose may have little or no relation to the first one. It did not appear that any demonstration was intended or made against Americans. A Spanish lady, an apologist for the riot, told me that it was begun by young Spanish army officers who were stung by insinuations or insults published by the Havana press against the Spanish army in Cuba. In the same spirit that leads students to occasionally redress a wrong excitedly and by force, the young Spaniards made an attack on the newspaper offices; citizens then took part, and the trouble grew beyond the intention of those who began it.

LIEUTENANT-COMMANDER ADOLPH MARIX, FORMER EXECUTIVE
OFFICER OF THE "MAINE"

Our Reception at Havana

While at Key West I was directed by the Navy Department to assist the collector of that port in operating against filibustering expeditions, I being senior officer present during the whole visit. At that time the Spanish press was indignant because it assumed that the United States was doing nothing to put a stop to filibustering. Certainly the American public had far more ground for indignation; it was almost impossible to put a complete stop to filibustering where there were so many bases of operation as existed along the Florida reefs and on the coasts north of them. It was generally the case that when an expedition was able to leave the United States, it landed in Cuba according to schedule. At one time five vessels engaged in watching for filibusters were in touch with the *Maine* by telegraph; and the *Maine's* steam-launches, as well as the *Marblehead's* launches, were out at night, bringing-to vessels moving out of Key West harbor. We did our work conscientiously.

At Key West I both accepted and gave a few luncheons or dinners. People from ashore appear to enjoy shipboard entertainments beyond reason as conceived by those who entertain afloat; novelty garnishes the feast, I suppose. John R. Bell, my cabin steward, was a "character"—one of the lovable, old-fashioned sort of "colored folks." He had not much merit as a chef, excepting that he could always find delicate lettuce, even, it seemed, where it had never before been known. He was honest to the core, and true to his duties. I never knew him to give himself any pleasure on shore, excepting the sad one of decorating the grave of a naval officer whom he had loved and served. It was impossible to find fault with him without punishing one's self. One could object to his acts only by delicate suggestion or kindly subterfuge. Periodically he would make me a pound-cake. I would cut from it a single slice, which I would secretly throw away. The cake would then adorn my sideboard in its remaining integrity for many days, to Bell's evident pride. His range of desserts was small. When he felt that he had run through his gamut, and needed time to think, he would make me an apple-pie, a colossal monstrosity that I abhorred. I would eat of his apple-pie — the same pie — day after day until it neared its end, when immunity would be claimed on the ground of its extreme richness. It was Bell's habit to agree with me before I had fully expressed any wish or thought. He would agree with me audibly at every stage of a verbal direction. There were noble deeds known to

Our Reception at Havana

me that he had done secretly year after year. No man can do more than his uttermost best, and that old Bell did habitually, according to his simple understanding.

I had been to Key West many times, but not since 1878. In the meantime the city had grown and had polished itself amazingly. Formerly orders to visit Key West were regarded as nearly equivalent to confinement to the ship. The place had no attraction in itself, and there was hardly any exchange of courtesies between the residents and the naval officers. The market offered little but fish and turtle. But during the *Maine's* visit we had a most agreeable time, and made the acquaintance of many people. The city had decidedly "gone into society." Young naval officers were beginning to marry there, and with good reason, according to my view of the matrimonial market. Various cities, in turn, have appeared to hold the monopoly of naval marriages, notably Norfolk, Virginia, Portsmouth, New Hampshire, and Erie, Pennsylvania. Why not Key West, by way of geographical distribution?

On Christmas eve, and again on Christmas night, the *Maine* was illuminated with hundreds of electric lights, to the great delight of the people of Key West, very few of whom had ever seen such a display. The arrangement of the

Maine's lights was worked out on board. It appeared to be generally conceded that it was surpassed only by that of the *Brooklyn*, which had been made at a navy-yard for Queen Victoria's Jubilee. The *Maine's* lights were strung fore and aft in a double rainbow, from bow to stern, and across the mastheads and funnels. There was also a row of lights completely encircling the ship along the ridge-rope of the awnings, which was at the height of the superstructure-deck. The following is quoted from one of the local newspapers:

"The beautiful illumination of the battle-ship *Maine*, on Christmas eve and night, was one of the finest displays of electricity ever witnessed in the city, or perhaps in the South. Hundreds of incandescent lights from the bow to the stern, up the masts and funnel, and around the ship's sides, made her one mass of lights. It was a picture not often seen in the tropical regions."

It became known after a time that the other large vessels of the North Atlantic Squadron, under command of Rear-Admiral Sicard, were to come to the waters about Key West for fleet drills and evolutions. At that time of year it was impracticable to have the drills elsewhere. The United States could not afford to abandon its best winter drill-ground for no other reason

CAPTAIN CROWNINSHIELD (DURING THE SPANISH WAR A MEMBER OF THE NAVAL BOARD) RECEIVING MR HERBERT, THEN SECRETARY OF THE NAVY, ON BOARD THE "MAINE."

than its proximity to Cuba. The squadron came and had its drills, as intended, but until war was opened never went nearer to Cuba than Key West and Tortugas, nor, so far as my knowledge goes, was it ever intended that it should.

During our visit to Key West I had inquired as to the best pilot for the reefs. There was a general concurrence of opinion that Captain Smith was the best man. He held himself subject to my call during our whole stay at Key West, when I might have been obliged to go out at night with the search-lights. Very few vessels of the *Maine's* draft had ever entered Key West harbor, for the reason that there is not enough water inside to allow deep-draft vessels to swing clear of their anchors. The bottom is hard, so anchors do not bury. There is no great difficulty in piloting, except that it is advisable to hold rigidly to the channel, which is narrow, so far as its depth has been tested by vessels passing through. The danger to be feared arises from the possibility of striking detached "coral heads" that have not been detected in the surveys that have been charted. A number of these heads at Key West and Tortugas have been discovered by the contact with them of United States men-of-war. The squadron was duly reported off Jupiter Inlet, on its passage south. We knew, therefore, at Key West, very nearly the hour when it would arrive off the reefs. The *Maine* had received orders to join the squadron when it appeared. It arrived off the reefs on Sunday, January 23, 1898. I sent ashore for our pilot, who in response was obliged to report that the pilot commissioners refused to let him take the *Maine* out, because their local rule of precedence required that the pilot who brought us in should by right take us out. I appealed against this rule as being merely one of local convenience or comfort, out of all proportion to the value of the *Maine* and the important public interests involved. The board of pilot commissioners weakened not — neither did I. The *Maine* went out without a pilot; so somebody lost nearly one hundred and fifty dollars, which remained in the coffers of the United States. While passing out I made sketches and copious notes of all the ranges and bearings used by the *Maine*, intending to formulate them and send them to the commander-in-chief, in the hope of relieving others of our vessels from petty and vexatious rules. My sketches and notes were lost with the *Maine*. After the departure of the *Maine*, the torpedo-boat *Cushing*, Lieutenant Albert

Our Reception at Havana

Gleaves, was charged with the maintenance of communication with General Lee.

On Sunday, the squadron, which included the *New York*, *Iowa*, *Massachusetts*, *Indiana*, and *Texas*, arrived off Key West. These vessels were joined by the *Maine*, *Montgomery*, and *Detroit*, from Key West harbor. When I went on board the flagship *New York* to report to Admiral Sicard, he looked so ill that I was greatly pleased at having ordered in advance all the arrangements at Key West that were deemed by him necessary to maintain and report communications with General Lee. Continued ill health made it necessary, about a month afterward, for Admiral Sicard to relinquish the command of the United States naval force on the North Atlantic station. It was only natural that I should greatly regret the detachment of Admiral Sicard. He had done me the honor to suggest that I take command of his flagship on the detachment of Captain Silas Casey, when the latter concluded his tour of sea service. After long consideration, I requested permission to decline the command of the *New York*, for the reason that there was a greater field for the acquirement and exercise of professional skill in a separate command. Underlying my declination was also the hope that I might, ultimately, reach Havana with the *Maine*.

The "Maine"

That night the squadron, eight vessels in all, remained at anchor outside the reefs off Sand Key light. The next day it got under way, and steamed west for Tortugas. In the afternoon we sighted a large English steamer aground on the reef to the westward of Sand Key. She signaled for immediate assistance. The *Detroit* was sent to aid her, and the remainder of the squadron stood on. About 6 P. M. the squadron anchored for the night on the bank, about ten miles to the southward of the southeastern entrance to Tortugas Roads. After anchoring, the vessels were directed by signal to bank fires. Approximately at nine o'clock, while all the vessels were engaged in receiving night-signals from the flagship, the *Maine*, which was occupying an easterly berth, sighted a vessel to the eastward making Very's signals to attract attention. The flagship, being well to the westward, did not see her for a long time. From the disposition of the lights shown by the arriving vessel, it was evident that she was of a very low free-board and very narrow beam. This, with her high speed of approach, convinced me that she was a torpedo-boat coming from Key West. I surmised that she was coming with despatches for the commander-in-chief. It occurred to me, also, that she was bringing orders for the *Maine* to go to Havana. It

THE "MAINE" ENTERING HAVANA HARBOR, MORRO CASTLE ON THE RIGHT.

was an intuition, but nothing more. Without waiting for a signal from the commander-in-chief, I ordered fires spread and preparations made for getting the *Maine* under way. The gig was also lowered and manned. The stranger proved to be the torpedo-boat *Dupont*, commanded by Lieutenant Spencer S. Wood. She reached the flagship about a half-hour after we had sighted her. Then there was an interval of suspense, which was concluded by a signal made from the flagship for the *Maine* to prepare to get under way, and for her commanding officer to report on board the flagship. The *Maine* at once replied, "All ready." I was in my gig and away almost before the signals were answered. It was a very dark night. The sea was rough and the tidal current strong. Suddenly the *Dupont* appeared right ahead of the gig, as if she had risen out of the sea. Her one visible light almost blinded me. She had seen us, but we had not sighted her until close under her bow. We made fast alongside. I went on board, and then sent the gig back to the *Maine*. The *Dupont* steamed near the flagship, which vessel sent a boat for me. There was more rough work in boarding the *New York*. I reported to the commander-in-chief, in obedience to signal.

Admiral Sicard announced that he had received instructions from the Navy Department to send

The "Maine"

the *Maine* to Havana. I do not know personally the precise reason which induced the United States government to act at that particular time.

On the 24th of January, the day during which the events just recorded took place, General Lee received the following telegram from the Department of State at Washington:

> It is the purpose of this government to resume the friendly naval visits at Cuban ports. In that view, the *Maine* will call at the port of Havana in a day or two. Please arrange for the friendly interchange of calls with the authorities.

On the afternoon of the 24th, General Lee went to the palace and notified the authorities and read the telegram to them. Immediately after receiving the telegram, however, he sent the following reply to the Department of State:

> Advise visit be postponed six or seven days to give last excitement time to disappear. Will see authorities, and let you know. Governor-general away for two weeks. I should know day and hour visit.

In the morning of the 25th, only a short time before the arrival of the *Maine* in Havana, General Lee sent the following telegram:

> At an interview, authorities profess to think United States has ulterior purpose in sending ship. Say it will obstruct autonomy, produce excitement, and most probably a demonstra-

Our Reception at Havana

tion. Ask that it is not done until they can get instructions from Madrid, and say that if for friendly purpose, as claimed, delay unimportant.

After the arrival of the *Maine*, General Lee telegraphed to the Department of State as follows:

> Ship quietly arrived, 11 A. M. to-day; no demonstration so far.

The same day he received from the Department of State the following telegram, dated the 24th:

> *Maine* has been ordered. Will probably arrive at Havana some time to-morrow, Tuesday. Cannot tell hour. Possibly early. Coöperate with the authorities for her friendly visit. Keep us advised by frequent telegrams.

My orders were to proceed to Havana and make a friendly visit. I was left to act according to my own judgment in the usual way; that is to say, it was undoubtedly assumed that I would know how to act on my arrival in Havana, and it was intended to hold me responsible for my action. The situation seemed to call for nothing more than a strictly careful adherence to the well-known forms of naval procedure and courtesy. It was to be expected that the Spanish people in Havana would prefer that the *Maine* should stay away; but with a lingering insurrection, the end of which was not in sight, with American interests in Cuba affected adversely,

The "Maine"

and American citizens in Cuba alarmed for their safety, the United States had decided to show its flag from a public vessel in Cuban waters. It is quite certain that I gave myself no concern over the diplomatic peculiarities of the situation. My vessel was selected to go to Havana, and I was gratified at the choice, just as any other commanding officer would have been. I volunteered the remark to Admiral Sicard that I should try to make no mistakes.

I rejoined the *Maine* by the same means that had been employed to reach the flagship. The *Maine* got under way about 11 P. M., and stood to the southward into the Gulf Stream. I wrote a long order in the night order-book relating to preparatory work to be done on the morning watch, and then turned in for the night. I did not desire to reach Havana at early daylight, but rather to steam in when the town was alive and on its feet; therefore a landfall was made at daylight the next morning, well to the westward. That was on Tuesday, January 25. The vessel was then slowed down and the decks were straightened up, so that she might present the usual orderly appearance for port. The crew was required to dress with exceptional neatness in blue; the officers were in frock-coats. When all was ready, the *Maine* was headed to

Wreck of *Maine*. Machina and boat-landing. *Vizcaya*. *Fern*.

VIEW OF HAVANA HARBOR FROM A WHARF IN REGLA.—I.

the eastward, nearly parallel to the shore-line of the city, and toward the entrance. She was sent ahead at full speed as she passed the city, and the United States national ensign was hoisted at the peak, and the "jack" at the foremast-head. This disclosed at once the nationality and purpose of the vessel; that is to say, the *Maine* was a United States man-of-war that desired a pilot to enter Havana harbor. All pilotage in and out of Havana, or within the harbor, is under the direction of the captain of the port, who is a naval officer. The pilot service is entirely official.

No United States vessel had visited Havana during the previous three years. There was much doubt as to the nature of our reception — to me, at least, there was doubt, for I was not aware of the character of the diplomatic exchanges. I was sincerely desirous of a friendly reception, but it was my affair to be ready for all emergencies. The *Maine* was in such a state of preparation that she could not have been taken at much disadvantage; nevertheless, she presented no offensive appearance, and meant no offense. On board United States men-of-war it is commonly only a short step from peaceful appearance to complete readiness.

A pilot put off promptly to the *Maine*, and

The "Maine"

boarded her to seaward of the Morro quite in the normal way, without objection or unusual inquiry. He took her in through the narrow entrance slowly, and with such care and excellent skill that I complimented him for it after we were made fast to the buoy. I also commended him to the captain of the port later. The forts, shores, and wharves were crowded with soldiers and citizens. A few riflemen could have cleared our decks when in the narrow entrance and under the shadow of the lofty Morro and Cabaña. Whatever feeling there was against us was kept in check by the populace. There were then in the harbor, moored to permanent mooring-buoys, two other men-of-war: the Spanish cruiser *Alfonso XII*, which never changed her position, from the time the *Maine* arrived until the *Maine* was sunk; and the square-rigged German training-steamer *Gniesenau*. The *Maine* moved slowly in, passing between the two men-of-war, and was moored to a mooring-buoy chosen by the pilot, about four hundred yards south of the German vessel in the man-of-war anchorage off the Machina or Naval "Sheers." She never left this buoy, but carried it down with her when she sank. It was approximately in the position of buoy No. 5, as shown on chart No. 307, published by the United States Hydrographic Of-

Our Reception at Havana

fice, but was known at Havana as buoy No. 4. At the time of the explosion of the *Maine*, the Spanish despatch-boat *Legazpi* occupied the berth which had been held formerly by the *Gniesenau*, buoy No. 3; the *Alfonso XII* was at No. 4 of Chart 307. The day after the arrival of the *Maine*, the square-rigged German training-steamer *Charlotte* entered the harbor. Other vessels were anchored or moored in localities more or less remote from the *Maine* — two hundred yards and upward.

Probably no forms of etiquette are more stable than those observed among navies in reciprocating courtesies. They are laid down in the navy regulations, and are established by rigid international convention. Those relating to reciprocal courtesies between naval ships and military and civil authorities are quite as well established; they are known in all ports much frequented by naval vessels. On the arrival of a foreign vessel in port, the senior naval officer present of the nation to which the port belongs sends an officer of the rank of lieutenant, or below, to the commanding officer of the arriving vessel, with an offer of civilities, or to express the wish of the naval authorities to give any assistance in their power. On the departure of the officer who makes this "visit of ceremony," an officer of the arriving vessel is

The "Maine"

promptly despatched to acknowledge the visit and to express the thanks of his commanding officer. The next step, in respect to visits, is for the commanding officer of the arriving vessel to call on the commanding officers of and above his own rank in the navy of the nation to which the port belongs. These visits must be returned, by convention, within twenty-four hours. It is also customary to visit the highest civil officer and the highest military officer. By these forms of naval ceremony, I was required to make visits at Havana to the captain-general (who is also governor-general), the Spanish admiral in charge of the station, the captain of the port, and the captain of the *Alfonso XII*. Visits are also exchanged in the United States service between the captain of an arriving man-of-war and the consular representative of the United States. General Fitzhugh Lee, as consul-general, was entitled to the first visit.

In command of the *Maine* at Havana, I had but one wish, which was to be friendly to the Spanish authorities, as required by my orders. I took pleasure in carrying out my orders in this respect, and sacrificed every personal inclination and promise of pleasure that might have interfered. The first Spanish officer to come on board was a naval lieutenant who represented the cap-

Harbor entrance. *Alfonso XII.* Cabanas.
Ojeando.
VIEW OF HAVANA HARBOR FROM A WHARF IN REGLA.—II.

tain of the port. His bearing was both dignified and polite (which, by the way, is invariably the rule with Spanish naval officers), but I thought he looked embarrassed and even humiliated in carrying out his duty. I greatly regretted that such should be the case, and did all that I could to make him feel at ease. After the arrival of a second Spanish lieutenant, who seemed to take matters more philosophically, and of a German naval lieutenant, the naval officer who had arrived first appeared to lose his embarrassment. I made all the visits required of me by usage, and was everywhere received with courtesy. It is hardly to the point whether there was any great amount of actual friendliness for us beneath the surface. The Spanish officials on every hand gave us absolutely all the official courtesy to which we were entitled by usage, and they gave it with the grace of manner which is characteristic of their nation. I accepted it as genuine.

It is not essential to enter here into the details of usage in connection with gun salutes. It is enough to say that convention required the *Maine* to salute the Spanish national flag, and also to salute Admiral Manterola. But such salutes are given only when it is known that they will be returned. I therefore deemed it prudent to determine this point, although the visit of a Spanish officer to the ship would ordinarily be thought sufficiently convincing. In the course of conversation with the Spanish naval officer who was the first to visit the *Maine*, I said: "I am about to give myself the honor of saluting your national flag; from which battery will the salute be returned?" He replied: "From the Cabaña." With that assurance, both salutes were fired and returned. The salute to the Spanish admiral was returned by his flagship, the *Alfonso XII*.

Shortly after the arrival of the *Maine*, I sent my aid, Naval Cadet J. H. Holden, ashore to report to General Lee, and announce that I would soon follow. I gave orders that no officers or men of the vessel should go ashore, unless by my express order. It was desired first to test public feeling, private and official, with reference to the *Maine's* visit. My visit to Admiral Manterola was made in full dress, with cocked hat, epaulets, etc. I landed at the Machina, the man-of-war landing, which is virtually at the Spanish admiral's residence. There was a crowd assembled, but only of moderate size. There was no demonstration of any kind; the crowd closed in about me slightly. I thought the people stolid and sullen, so far as I could gather from an occasional glance, but I took very little notice of anybody. On my return, however, I noted carefully

Our Reception at Havana

the bearing of the various groups of Spanish soldiers that I passed. They saluted me, as a rule, but with so much expression of apathy that the salute really went for nothing. Some members of a group would salute, while others would not. They made no demonstration against me, however, not even by look.

The same day I made my visit to General Lee, and arranged with him for my visit to the acting captain- and governor-general, who at that time was General Parrado, Captain-General Blanco being absent on a tour of the island. It is customary in the case of high officials to make the visit at an appointed time. When I made my visit, on January 27, accompanied by General Lee, there seemed at first to be a probability of embarrassment. We called at the palace of General Blanco at the appointed time, and apparently nobody there knew anything about our appointment. The ever-present American newspaperman relieved the situation; he ascertained that General Parrado was in a residence across the way, where he was expecting us. We promptly repaired the mistake, and were received by General Parrado with great courtesy. He had a table spread with refreshments for our benefit. All of my official visits were returned promptly. General Parrado returned my visit in person, and was given the salute of a captain- and governor-general; that is to say, of the governor of a colony — seventeen guns, the same salute which is prescribed for the governor of one of the United States.

All visits were made without friction and with courtesy on both sides, and apparently with all the freedom of conversation and action usually observed. I showed General Parrado through the *Maine*, and he seemed much pleased.

It had been announced in the local newspapers that there would be a series of bull-fights in Havana, in which would appear Mazzantini, the famous "gentleman bull-fighter of Spain." I had decided to go to a bull-fight, notwithstanding the day of its celebration was Sunday. I was anxious to know from my own observation the true feeling of the people of Havana toward the *Maine*. Learning that the common people were likely to be greatly excited at the bull-fight, I decided that my presence there would afford the very best opportunity for my purpose. I told General Parrado of my intention, and he at once offered me a box. I declined the offer, saying that some of the officers of the *Maine* and I would go simply as ordinary observers. However, within a day or two, General Parrado sent me tickets for a box, which was an act of kind-

THE "MAINE" SALUTING THE SPANISH FLAG AFTER MAKING FAST TO THE OFFICIAL BUOY AT WHICH SHE WAS DESTROYED.

Our Reception at Havana

ness greatly appreciated by us. Later he sent a case of fine sherry to the officers of the *Maine*. The *Maine* had been for so long away from our large cities that I lacked anything distinctly American that would have been appropriate to give to General Parrado to express in a reciprocal way our appreciation of his gift, so I sent him, with the best of good wishes, a copy of my own work on "Deep-Sea Sounding and Dredging," published by the United States Coast Survey in 1880.

On the first Sunday after the arrival of the *Maine* at Havana, General Lee gave a luncheon-party to the officers of the ship, at the Havana Yacht-Club at Marianao, a place on the sea-shore, about eight miles west of Havana. There we met some Cuban gentlemen, one or two members of foreign consulates, and a number of press correspondents. In going there I was taken by the sea route, in a small steam-launch owned by one of the Cuban gentlemen. We went close alongshore, past all the batteries west of the entrance. There was no impropriety in this, because one could see the batteries to better advantage merely by driving along one of the most frequented driveways of the city. At Marianao there was a small Spanish garrison. Sentries were posted at various places, and at one time, I believe, they

The "Maine"

had occupied the roof of the club-house. There was no excitement or even special interest shown by the soldiers at the appearance there of United States officers. The entertainment passed off very pleasantly. General Lee toasted the naval party, and we toasted General Lee. Short complimentary speeches were made on each side.

The box at the bull-fight which had been provided us by the courtesy of General Parrado contained six seats. I reserved one ticket for General Lee, one for Naval Cadet Holden, and one for myself. The other three I sent to the ward-room and the junior officers' mess, to be chosen by lot. The party, therefore, consisted of six people. We returned to Havana from the yacht-club by train, and could not help remarking the suitability of the country for guerrilla warfare. While we were yet in the train, an American gentleman discussed with us the propriety of going to the bull-fight. He explained that the common people on such occasions were generally greatly excited, and as our visit to Havana was not well regarded by the populace, there was a probability that one single cry against us might set the audience aflame. I believed that it was inconsistent with the friendly visit of the *Maine* that her officers should not be accorded the same freedom of appearance and

LUNCHEON GIVEN AT THE HAVANA YACHT CLUB AT 11 A. M., JANUARY 30, 1898, BY UNITED STATES CONSUL-GENERAL FITZHUGH LEE, TO THE CAPTAIN AND OFFICERS OF THE U. S. S. "MAINE."

Our Reception at Havana

action that was permitted to officers of other navies, therefore I reasserted our intention to go. Our friend said: "Well, if they will allow you there, they will allow you anywhere."

As we emerged from the train and passed out of the station on our arrival at Havana, I was handed by somebody (I think by one of the newspaper correspondents) the bellicose circular which has since been published in the newspapers. It was a small printed sheet containing a protest to the public against submission to a visit from the *Maine*, and, translated, reads as follows:

SPANIARDS!

LONG LIVE SPAIN WITH HONOR!

What are you doing that you allow yourselves to be insulted in this way? Do you not see what they have done to us in withdrawing our brave and beloved Weyler, who at this very time would have finished with this unworthy, rebellious rabble who are trampling on our flag and on our honor?

Autonomy is imposed on us to cast us aside and give places of honor and authority to those who initiated this rebellion, these low-bred autonomists, ungrateful sons of our beloved country!

And, finally, these Yankee pigs who meddle in our affairs, humiliating us to the last degree, and, for a still greater taunt, order to us a man-of-war of their rotten squadron, after insulting us in their newspapers with articles sent from our own home!

Spaniards! the moment of action has arrived. Do not go

¡Españoles!

¡VIVA ESPAÑA CON HONRA!

¿Qué haceis que os dejais insultar de esa manera? ¿No veis lo que nos han hecho retirando á nuestro valiente y querido Weyler, que á estas horas ya hubiéramos acabado con esta indigna canalla insurrecta que pisotea nuestra bandera y nuestro honor?

Nos imponen la Autonomía para echarnos á un lado y dar los puestos de honor y mando á aquellos que iniciaron esta rebelion, estos mal nacidos autonomistas, hijos ingratos de nuestra querida patria!

Y por último, estos cochinos yankees que se mezclan en nuestros asuntos, humillándonos hasta el último grado, y para más vejámen nos mandan uno de los barcos de guerra de su  podrida escuadra, despues de insultarnos en sus diarios y desde nuestra casa!

Españoles! Llegó el momento de accion, no dormiteis! Enseñemos á esos viles traidores que todavía no hemos perdido la vergüenza y que sabemos protestar con la energía que corresponde á una nacion digna y fuerte como es y siempre será nuestra España!

Mueran los americanos! Muera la Autonomía!
Viva España! Viva Weyler!

FACSIMILE OF THE CIRCULAR HANDED TO CAPTAIN SIGSBEE ON HIS WAY TO THE BULL-FIGHT AND LATER SENT TO HIM THROUGH THE HAVANA POST-OFFICE.

The words underscored, with the hand pointing to them, mean "rotten squadron."

Our Reception at Havana

to sleep! Let us teach these vile traitors that we have not yet lost our pride, and that we know how to protest with the energy befitting a nation worthy and strong, as our Spain is, and always will be!

Death to the Americans!   Death to autonomy!
Long live Spain!   Long live Weyler!

I put it in my pocket, and we went to the bull-fight by means of the ferry plying between Havana and Regla. I have been asked many times what I thought of the circular. At the time I thought it of no importance whatever, and I have not changed my opinion. It could only have been the screaming appeal of some bigoted and impotent patriot. When a would-be conspirator finds it necessary thus to go out into the public streets and beg anonymously for assistance, he demonstrates that he is without friends of executive spirit. Circulars of that kind are not uncommon in Havana. General Lee received them frequently. In his case, the date was generally set for his destruction. He gave himself no concern over them, but let it be known generally that any one attempting to injure him bodily would be treated very summarily by himself. His poise in matters of that kind made murderous bulletins positively humorous.

There had formerly been a bull-ring in Havana, a well-appointed one, but for some reason it was closed, and the smaller ring at Regla, across the bay from Havana, had taken its place. When we arrived at the ring, we found that our box was high up above the rows of seats, and close to the box occupied by General Parrado, who was the presiding official at the sport on that day. Members of his staff were with him. Stationed at intervals throughout the audience were individual soldiers, under arms, and there were about twenty assembled in the seat directly in front of our box. General Parrado bowed to me pleasantly, but I thought that he and the officers about him were not entirely free from embarrassment because of our presence. General Parrado was always especially kind in his intercourse with me. I felt very friendly toward him. Occasionally, on looking up suddenly, I detected glances at me, on one side or another, that were far from friendly. That was to have been expected; but on the whole the forbearance of the audience was remarkable and commendable.

Six bulls were killed during the day. Our party arrived as the first one was being hauled away dead. After the fifth bull had been despatched, it was decided, as a considerate measure in favor of General Parrado, that we should leave the building and return to Havana early, so as to avoid the crowd. We therefore left very quietly, just before the sixth bull entered the ring. We tried to reach the ferry promptly, so that we might return to Havana on a steamer having but few passengers. Three members of our party were successful in this attempt; but General Lee, Lieutenant Holman, and I failed. On our arrival, a steamer had just left the landing. We then hailed a small passenger-boat, and were pulled to the *Maine*. While General Lee and I were conversing on the quarter-deck of the *Maine*, a ferry-boat came across the bay, carrying back to Havana a large number of people from the audience. There was no demonstration of any kind. The passengers were doubtless those who had left early, hoping, like ourselves, to avoid the crowd. The next ferry-boat was densely crowded. Among the passengers were a number of officers of the Spanish army and of the volunteers. As the ferry-boat passed the *Maine* there were derisive calls and whistles. Apparently not more than fifty people participated in that demonstration. It was not general, and might have occurred anywhere. I have never believed that the Spanish officers or soldiers took part. It is but fair to say that this was the only demonstration of any kind made against the *Maine* or her officers, either collectively or individually, so far as was made known to me, during our visit.

The "Maine"

Adverse feeling toward us was shown by the apathetic bearing of soldiers when they saluted, or of tradesmen when they supplied our needs. After the *Maine* had been sunk, and when the *Montgomery* and the *Fern* were in Havana, Spanish passenger-boatmen exhibited bad temper by withholding or delaying answers to our hails at night. The failure of the Spanish authorities to compel the boatmen to answer our hails impressed me as being very closely akin to active unfriendliness. It was at the time when the *Vizcaya* and the *Oquendo* were in Havana, using picket-boats and occasionally search-lights at night, apparently to safeguard themselves. Hails were made sharply and answered promptly between the Spanish men-of-war and the boats constantly plying about the harbor at night. It must have been plain on board the Spanish men-of-war that the boatmen were trifling with us. This was after the *Vizcaya* had visited New York.

The feeling of moral responsibility in the United States for the safety of the visiting Spanish cruiser, as against a belief that she would be molested, is exemplified in Appendix B, which contains an extract from the New York "Herald" of February 19, 1898.

I have been taken to task on some sides in the United States for going to a bull-fight on Sun-

CAPTAIN SIGSBEE, GENERAL FITZHUGH LEE, SEVERAL OFFICERS OF THE "MAINE," AND CIVILIANS AT THE HAVANA YACHT-CLUB.

Our Reception at Havana

day. Perhaps I should confess that I attended two bull-fights in Havana, on successive Sundays, that being the only day, I believe, on which bull-fights take place. On the second occasion I went with an American friend and a party of Cuban gentlemen who stood well with the Spaniards. This visit was neither attended nor followed by any demonstration unfavorable to Americans or the *Maine*. We entered, remained, and left quite in the usual way. Two bull-fights exhausted all interest that I felt to see that historic sport. The love for domestic animals which is part of an American's nature — ingrained from babyhood — revolts at the sight of a poor, non-combatant horse calmly obeying the bridle while his entrails are streaming from him. To comprehend the Spanish bull-fight, it should be considered as a savage sport passed down from generation to generation from a remote period when human nature was far more cruel than at present. If the sport had not so developed, it is a fair inference that it could not now be instituted or tolerated. Similar considerations might be thought to apply to our own prize-fights; but the highest class of people habitually attends bull-fights, while this is not true of prize-fights. During the progress of the last bull-fight that I attended, several poor, docile, passive horses were killed under circumstances that were shocking to the American mind. In a box near that which my friends and I occupied, a little girl ten or twelve years of age sat apparently unmoved while a horse was prostrate and dying in prolonged agony near the middle of the ring.

As to the circular that was given to me before going to the first bull-fight, it may be stated that I received a second copy through the Havana mail. The second copy was probably sent by some American who judged it to be important. I sent it home, and afterward it was reproduced in the newspapers. It is reproduced here. I think General Lee sent a copy of that circular to the secretary-general of Cuba, Dr. Congosto. There was nothing to do in respect to the circular, even though I had believed it an influential attempt to foment disturbance. Every precaution that could be taken against injury or treachery was taken on board the *Maine*, so far as could be permitted under the restrictions of my orders requiring me to make a friendly visit. If one, when dining with a friend at his home, were to test the dishes for poison, he would not be making a friendly visit. The harbor could not be dragged without giving offense; it could not be patrolled by our own picket-boats at night, nor could the search-lights be kept going: but every internal precaution was exercised that the situation suggested. There were sentries on the forecastle and poop, quartermaster and signal-boy on the bridge, and a second signal-boy on the poop, all of whom were charged with the necessity for a careful lookout. The corporal of the guard was specially instructed as to the port gangway, and the officer of the deck and the quartermaster as to the starboard gangway.

Instead of the usual anchor-watch, a quarter-watch was kept on deck at night. The sentries were supplied with ammunition; a number of rounds of rapid-fire ammunition were kept in the pilot-house and in the spare captain's pantry inside the after-superstructure. An additional supply of shells was kept at hand for the six-inch guns. In order to be prepared more completely to work the hydraulic mechanism of the turrets, steam was kept up on two boilers instead of one; special instructions were given to watch all the details of the hydraulic gear and to report defects. The officer of the deck was charged by me to make detailed reports, even in minor matters, acting on the suspicion that we might be in an unfriendly harbor. I personally instructed the master-at-arms and the orderly sergeant to keep a careful eye on every visitor that came on board, and to charge their own subordinates to

The "Maine"

the same purpose. I instructed them to follow visitors about at a proper distance whenever the ship was visited below; they were carefully to watch for any packages that might be laid down or left by visitors, on the supposition that dynamite or other high explosives might be used. They were also required to inspect the routes over which visitors had passed. The officer in charge of the marine guard was required to make at least two visits during the night to the various posts of the vessel. The dipping lines or hogging-lines of the collision mat — a large mat to haul over holes, under water, in the hull — were rove and kept standing. The purport of my own orders and instructions was that we should consider the *Maine* in a position demanding extreme vigilance, and requiring a well-sustained routine both by day and by night.

Until the night of the explosion nothing whatever was developed to show that there was any special need for extreme vigilance. Many people visited the ship, chiefly in parties. It is probable that nearly all were Cubans. These were chiefly representatives of the refined class in Havana, who took great pride in visiting the ship — more, perhaps, than I could have wished, in view of the situation. There must have been three or four hundred of them on board from

CAPTAIN SIGSBEE IN THE CAPTAIN'S CABIN ON BOARD THE "MAINE."
The Admiral's cabin, similarly arranged, is seen to the right through the open, wide doorway.

time to time. They were warmly demonstrative toward us, and at first were inclined to ask us to return their visits. I believe some of the *Maine's* officers took advantage of their invitations; but I always explained that my position in Havana was a delicate one, that I desired to know socially both the Spaniards and the Cubans, but that I should not feel free to accept hospitalities from Cubans until the Spanish people first showed a willingness to accept the hospitalities of the ship. I often made inquiries in a rather jocular way as to the politics of the ladies who visited the ship. The ladies pointed out to me visitors of different shades of opinion, but I have my doubts whether any of them were really in sympathy with the Spaniards. I let it be known everywhere that it would please me greatly to entertain the Spanish people on board, and made considerable effort to bring about the desired result, but without success. It was evident that the Spaniards would not visit us socially; they would do their official duty, but would not go beyond it.

I finally decided to make a very special effort. I knew two charming young Spanish ladies of American descent on their mother's side. Both were engaged to be married to Spanish army officers. Their father had been a Spanish officer. All their associations had been in Spanish military circles. They assured me that it was a mistake to suppose that the Spaniards would not visit us in a friendly way. To demonstrate their view, they offered to bring aboard the *Maine*, on a certain day, a party of Spanish officers. The ladies came at the appointed time, their mother being one of the party; but with them there was only one Spanish officer, and he was in what we might call a civil branch of the army. Each lady gave a somewhat different excuse for the absence of the officers, which only served to make it clear that the officers would not come at all, and that there was a general understanding that the ship should not be visited by Spanish officers, except officially.

I then believed that I had made all the effort that was proper to put the visit of the *Maine* on a friendly plane socially. I made no effort thereafter beyond continuing to make it known in a general way that Spaniards would be welcomed. For about two days after the arrival of the *Maine*, her officers were not permitted to go ashore; after that they went freely, day and night. During the whole visit the crew remained on board, with the exception of an occasional visit to the shore, on duty, by some well-trusted petty officer. I regretted very much to retain the crew on board, because it had been my cus-

Our Reception at Havana

tom to give liberty freely before visiting Havana. Even the bumboatmen did not seem to care especially for the custom of the men, doubtless because of the undercurrent of feeling against us. The crew never complained — not in a single instance that I am aware of; they took the situation philosophically. I myself drove through the streets of Havana, day or night, entirely alone, just as I liked, without hindrance of any kind. To all outward appearance Havana was as orderly a city as I have ever seen.

It was impossible to be at Havana without hearing much about reconcentrados. I never spoke of them to Spanish officials, but at different times conversed with non-military Spaniards on the subject. To my surprise, they were perfectly frank and outspoken in their admissions of the terrible suffering and death that had been wrought. The statistics that they gave me were not diminished as compared with those received from the Cubans; in fact, their figures were higher as a rule; but there was this difference: the Cubans placed the blame upon the Spaniards, and the Spaniards upon the Cubans. A Spanish lady, in speaking of General Weyler in connection with the reconcentrados, said of him that he was not a man of sentiment, but cold by nature, a soldier with a stern sense of duty.

The "Maine"

Prior to the destruction of the *Maine*, I was unwittingly involved in one case of official friction. According to precedents, I was entirely in the right. The autonomistic government of Cuba had been established by General Blanco. The members of the government were much-respected gentlemen of the island. As captain of the *Maine*, I was not expected to show any political preference, but it was my duty to preserve good relations with the government as it existed. In visiting the captain-general, who, as already stated, is also the governor-general, and the naval authorities, I thought I had fulfilled all the courtesies required by usage; therefore it had not occurred to me to visit the civil members of the autonomistic council. In my cruises about the West Indies, I had made visits to colonial governors and to the naval and military authorities; but it had never been expected of me to visit the members of the legislative council of a British colony. I was therefore greatly surprised to find that it had been reported to the United States government in Washington that I had failed to visit the members of the autonomistic council. I received several telegrams from the Navy Department referring to the matter. The despatches may not have been clearly deciphered on board the *Maine*, but I did not gather from them that I

THE WARDROOM OF THE "MAINE"

Lieutenant-Commander Marix, left foreground, was executive officer of the *Maine* when this photograph was made, but was detached before the explosion. He served as judge-advocate at the Court of Inquiry. Chaplain Chidwick stands in the middle background, and facing him is Lieutenant Jenkins, who was lost.

Our Reception at Havana

was required to make a visit to those officials. I hesitated to act without decisive orders after the matter had been carried to the government at Washington. Finally, I thought that I could detect in the telegrams a desire on the part of the Navy Department that I should, of my own volition, make the visit.

General Blanco had then returned to Havana, where he resumed his custom of giving receptions to gentlemen on a certain night in each week. General Lee had made an appointment for me to visit General Blanco officially the next day, and I took advantage of the reception to promote good feeling. In civilian's evening dress, I attended General Blanco's reception with General Lee, and took pleasure in the act. I said to General Blanco that I attended his reception that evening informally, and that I would come officially the following day, according to appointment. General Blanco is a fine type of the Spanish gentleman — a man of distinguished bearing and address. I remarked to General Lee that the captain-general might pass for a very benevolent United States senator. This was a double-edged compliment, intended to cut favorably in both directions. At the reception and on all other occasions General Blanco received me most kindly.

The "Maine"

Soon after our arrival at the reception, General Lee introduced me to Dr. Congosto, the secretary-general of Cuba. Dr. Congosto immediately said: "May I introduce you to the members of the autonomistic council?" I replied that the introduction would give me great pleasure, and that I should gladly have acted on an earlier invitation. I was then introduced to several members of the council, including Señor Galvaez, the president. All were men that one would feel honored to meet, whether officially or privately. I thought I had a right to speak plainly, because I had been put in a false position. I informed the gentlemen that there had been no time since my visit to Havana when I should not have given myself the honor of visiting them immediately had I received an intimation that a visit would be agreeable. I stated that I had not made a visit because no precedent for it in naval etiquette was known to me, and that visits to civil officials on shore, if in excess of usage, might not be taken kindly, because a return visit afloat might be inconvenient. I expressed the pleasure that I should take in going as far beyond precedent as might be agreeable to them. If permitted, I should visit the council officially the following day, after which I hoped the gentlemen of the council would visit the *Maine* and receive a salute.

Our Reception at Havana

The next day, with General Lee, I called on General Blanco officially, just as I had called on General Parrado when he was representing General Blanco. I admired General Blanco as a man and as a patriot, and desired to receive him on board the *Maine* and do him honor. I gave him an urgent invitation, stating at the same time that I knew it was not necessary etiquette for him to return my visit personally. He seemed pleased, and remarked pleasantly that there was a decree against captains-general visiting foreign men-of-war, for the reason that many years ago a captain-general, while visiting an English man-of-war, had been abducted. I replied that on merely personal grounds I would be glad to run away with him, but I promised good behavior. He stated that it might be possible to make a visit—he would think it over. I assured General Blanco that the visit of the *Maine* was sincerely friendly, and that my orders contemplated nothing further than the ordinary visit of a man-of-war. He expressed his appreciation of my commands against giving liberty on shore to the *Maine's* crew, and asked, as had other officials, how long the *Maine* would remain at Havana. To this question I always made the same reply, viz., that when our war-vessels were in telegraphic communication with the Navy Department it was not customary to include in their orders the time of their departure from a port; they were required to await further orders. I repeated to General Blanco what I had already said to General Parrado, that I hoped the Spanish men-of-war would reciprocate by reviving their friendly visits to the United States; that the cordiality of their reception could not be doubted. An exceptionally pleasing ceremonial feature terminates a visit to Spanish officials. It was observed in this case. After taking leave in the usual way, in the room where the interview was held, General Blanco and Dr. Congosto accompanied us to the head of the stairs, and the civilities were repeated. There they remained until we had reached the first landing below, when we turned, and the visit was ended by mutual salutation. After leaving General Blanco, I called on the members of the council, and was received with cordiality. I think the members of the autonomistic government had really felt that I was trying to evade a visit. I was glad to convince them to the contrary. It was well known to the authorities at Havana that General Lee had expressed officially an unfavorable opinion as to the influence and acceptability of autonomy in the island, and they were keenly sensitive on the subject. They may have believed that I was trying to weaken autonomy; if so, an invitation to visit the council would have made a test.

CAPTAIN-GENERAL RAMON BLANCO.

Our Reception at Havana

The gentlemen of the council returned my visit promptly. They were received with honors, and shown through the *Maine*. We greatly enjoyed their visit. Near the close, refreshments were served in my cabin, and Señor Galvaez made a complimentary speech in Spanish, which was interpreted to me briefly. The last thing that I desired was to involve myself in the politics of the island. I conceived that it would be highly injudicious on my part, as a foreign naval officer, to seem to take sides in any way, either by expression or by action. I made a response to Señor Galvaez's speech, assuring him that it had given me much gratification to make my visits to the council, and renewing my statement that I should have made an earlier visit had I known that it would have been agreeable. I welcomed them formally to the ship, and expressed the hope that they would return with their families and friends, and make social and informal visits whenever they thought they could find pleasure on board. Believing that the gentlemen of the council were desirous that I should give some expression of approval of the autonomistic form of government, I evaded the point, and said only: "I beg to express my admiration for the high purpose of your honorable body." My reply was afterward printed in at least two newspapers in Havana, but the terms made me favor autonomistic government for the island. I disliked this result when I considered it in connection with the censorship, but raised no protest against it. Judging from outward evidence, the autonomistic government was then unpopular and without effective influence, as reported by General Lee. My courtesy to the members of the council could hardly have gained popular favor for the *Maine*.

The next day the families and friends of the members of the council, including ladies, came aboard, and were received by me and the officers. It was a merry party, and many evidences of good will were given. This ended the only frictional incident prior to the destruction of the *Maine*.

While lying in the landlocked harbor of Havana, the *Maine* looked much larger than her actual size; she seemed enormous. Doubtless her strength was overestimated by the populace of Havana. The people apparently believed that we had sent our best ship to make a demonstration. There was much misconception on all sides, even among Spanish officers, as to the fighting strength of the United States navy. Evidently the Spaniards did not regard us as their equals in battle; their traditional pride made them overestimate their own fighting ability — or underestimate ours. On the other hand, to show how people may differ, I have never known it to be entertained in our own service that the Spanish navy could match ours. The Spanish naval officers that I met were alert, intelligent, and well informed professionally. They all had their polished national manner. Superficially, at least, their vessels were admirable; they seemed clean and well kept. Their etiquette was carefully observed, but apparently their crews were not comparable with ours, either in physique or in intelligence. I saw very little drilling of any kind on board the Spanish men-of-war at Havana. After the destruction of the *Maine*, General Weyler was credited in the press with the remark that "the *Maine* was indolent." If General Weyler did in fact make the remark, he must have got advices relative to the *Maine* that were not well based on observation. While at Havana, the *Maine* had no drills on shore, as a matter of course, but afloat she carried out her routine of drills day after day, except that she omitted "night quarters" and "clearing ship for action," as likely to give rise to misunderstanding. She also exercised her boats under oars and under sails, and had gun-pointing practice with the aid of a launch steaming about the harbor. In this latter practice, care was taken that our guns should never point toward the Spanish

The "Maine"

men-of-war. Every morning and evening the crew were put through the development drill. Most of the drills of the *Maine* were in plain view from without, by reason of her structure; she had no bulwarks on her main or upper deck.

After the destruction of the *Maine*, and while the *Vizcaya* and *Oquendo* were in the harbor, we could observe no drills taking place on board those vessels, although it is possible that they might have gone on without our being able to observe them. There was much ship-visiting on board. In everything they did, except in respect to etiquette, the practised nautical eye could not fail to note their inferiority in one degree or another to the vessels of our own squadron at Key West. Our vessels were then having "general quarters for action" three times a week, and were keeping up their other drills, including night-drills, search-light practice, etc. Vessels of the *Vizcaya* class, in the captain's cabin and officers' quarters, were one long stretch of beautiful woodwork, finer than is the rule on board our own vessels. The smaller guns of their primary batteries, and the rapid-firing guns of their secondary batteries, were disposed between the turrets on two decks in such dovetailed fashion that in order to do great damage an enemy needed only to hit anywhere in the region of the funnels. I

SIGNAL-DRILL ON THE DECK OF THE "MAINE."

Our Reception at Havana

remarked several times — once to Admiral Sampson, who was then Captain Sampson of the court of inquiry on the destruction of the *Maine* — that the Spanish vessels would be all aflame within ten minutes after they had gone into close action, and that their quarters at the guns would be a slaughter-pen. Future events justified the statement. Afterward, when I boarded the wreck of the *Infanta Maria Teresa* near Santiago de Cuba, her armored deck was below water, but above that there was not even a splinter of woodwork in sight; in fact, there was hardly a cinder left of her decks or of that beautiful array of bulkheads. It may have been that the *Maine* remained longer in Havana than had originally been intended by the Navy Department. It was expected, I believe, to relieve her by another vessel; which vessel, I do not know. I had hoped that the *Indiana* or the *Massachusetts* would be sent to dispel the prevailing ignorance among the Spanish people in regard to the strength and efficiency of our ships. The department may not have accepted my views.

Before reciting the details immediately connected with the destruction of the *Maine*, it may be said that I did not expect she would be blown up, either from interior or exterior causes, although precautions were taken in both directions.

The "Maine"

Nevertheless, I believed that she could be blown up from the outside, provided a sufficient number of persons of evil disposition, and with the conveniences at hand, were free to conspire for the purpose. It was necessary to trust the Spanish authorities in great degree for protection from without. I believe that the primary cause of the destruction of the *Maine* was an explosion under the bottom of the ship, as reported by the court of inquiry.

II

THE EXPLOSION

ON the night of the explosion, the *Maine*, lying in the harbor of Havana at the buoy where she was moored by the Spanish pilot on her entrance into the port, was heading in a direction quite unusual — at least, for the *Maine*. In this connection it should be explained that Havana is in the region of the trade-wind, which, however, is not so stable there as farther to the eastward, especially in the winter months. During the day the wind is commonly from the eastward, and about sundown it is likely to die down. During the night there may be no wind at all, and a ship swinging at her buoy may head in any direction. On the night of the explosion the *Maine* was heading to the northward and westward, in the general direction of the Machina, or naval "sheers," near the admiral's palace. Some of the watch-officers said afterward that they had not

The "Maine"

before known her to head in that direction at Havana. I myself did not remark any peculiarity of heading, because I had not been on deck much during the night-watches. Stated simply as a fact, the *Maine* was lying in the position in which she would have been sprung to open her batteries on the shore fortifications. If an expert had been charged with mining the *Maine's* mooring-berth, purely as a measure of harbor defense, and having only one mine available, it is believed that he would have placed it under the position that the *Maine* occupied that night.

A short distance astern, or nearly astern, was the American steamer *City of Washington*, Captain Frank Stevens, of the Ward line. The *Alfonso XII* and the *Legazpi* occupied the berths mentioned heretofore. They were on the starboard side of the *Maine*. There were other vessels in the harbor, but they were more remote from the *Maine's* berth. It was a dark, overcast night. The atmosphere was heavy, and the weather unusually hot and sultry.

THE MAINTOP.

The Stars and Stripes flying at half-mast over the wreck of the *Maine*, and above the flag is seen hanging from a line of the signal-yard a swab blown from the deck.

THE "MAINE" IN DRY-DOCK NO. 2, NEW YORK NAVY-YARD.

The Explosion

All of the twenty-six officers [1] were aboard excepting Passed Assistant Engineer F. C. Bowers, Naval Cadet (Engineer) Pope Washington, Paymaster's Clerk Brent McCarthy, and Gunner Joseph Hill.

The members of the crew, three hundred and twenty-eight in number, were on board as usual. One of the steam-launches was in the water, and riding at the starboard boom. The crew, excepting those on watch or on post, were turned in. The men of the quarter-watch were distributed about the deck in various places, wherever they could make themselves comfortable within permissible limits as to locality. Some of the officers were in their state-rooms or in the mess-rooms below; others were on the main or upper deck, in or about the officers' smoking-quarters, which were abaft the after-turret, on the port side, abreast the after-superstructure.

I was in my quarters, sitting on the after-side

---

[1] The officers of the *Maine* at the time were: captain, Charles D. Sigsbee; executive officer, Lieutenant-Commander Richard Wainwright; navigator, Lieutenant George F. W. Holman; lieutenants, John Hood and Carl W. Jungen; lieutenants, junior-grade, George P. Blow, John J. Blandin, and Friend W. Jenkins; naval cadets, Jonas H. Holden, Watt T. Cluverius, Amon Bronson, Jr., and David F. Boyd, Jr.; surgeon, Lucien G. Heneberger; paymaster, Charles M. Ray; chief engineer, Charles P. Howell; passed assistant engineer, Frederic C. Bowers; assistant engineers, John R. Morris and Darwin R. Merritt; naval cadets (engineer division), Pope Washington and Arthur Crenshaw; chaplain, John P. Chidwick; first lieutenant of marines, Albertus W. Catlin; boatswain, Francis E. Larkin; gunner, Joseph Hill; carpenter, George Helms; pay-clerk, Brent McCarthy.

of the table in the port or admiral's cabin. As previously stated, the *Maine* had been arranged to accommodate both an admiral and a captain. For this purpose her cabin space in the after-superstructure had been divided into two parts, starboard and port, which were perfectly symmetrical in arrangement and fittings. Looking from one cabin into the other through the large communicating doorway, one cabin was like the reflection of the other seen in a mirror. The two cabins were alike even in furniture. One of the illustrations in the book shows me sitting at the starboard-cabin table looking at the log-book. At the time of the explosion I was sitting in the port cabin in the corresponding position. The situation would be shown precisely if that illustration were reversed by reflection in a mirror.

About an hour before the explosion I had completed a report called for by Mr. Theodore Roosevelt, Assistant Secretary of the Navy, on the advisability of continuing to place torpedo-tubes on board cruisers and battle-ships. I then wrote a letter home, in which I struggled to apologize for having carried in my pocket for ten months a letter to my wife from one of her friends of long standing. The cabin mess-attendant, James Pinckney, had brought me, about an hour before, a civilian's thin coat, because of the prevailing

The Explosion

heat; I had taken off my blouse, and was wearing this coat for the only time during the cruise. In the pocket I had found the unopened and undelivered letter. Pinckney, a light-hearted colored man, who spent much of his spare time in singing, playing the banjo, and dancing jigs, was for some reason in an especially happy frame of mind that night. Poor fellow! he was killed, as was also good old John R. Bell, the colored cabin steward already referred to, who had been in the navy, in various ratings, for twenty-seven years.

At taps ("turn in and keep quiet"), ten minutes after nine o'clock, I laid down my pen to listen to the notes of the bugle, which were singularly beautiful in the oppressive stillness of the night. The marine bugler, Newton, who was rather given to fanciful effects, was evidently doing his best. During his pauses the echoes floated back to the ship with singular distinctness, repeating the strains of the bugle fully and exactly. A half-hour later, Newton was dead.

I was inclosing my letter in its envelop when the explosion came. The impression made on different people on board the *Maine* varied somewhat. To me, in my position, well aft, and within the superstructure, it was a bursting, rending, and crashing sound or roar of immense volume, largely metallic in character. It was followed by a succession of heavy, ominous, metallic sounds, probably caused by the overturning of the central superstructure and by falling debris. There was a trembling and lurching motion of the vessel, a list to port, and a movement of subsidence. The electric lights, of which there were eight in the cabin where I was sitting, went out. Then there was intense blackness and smoke.

The situation could not be mistaken: the *Maine* was blown up and sinking. For a moment the instinct of self-preservation took charge of me, but this was immediately dominated by the habit of command. I went up the inclined deck into the starboard cabin, toward the starboard air-ports, which were faintly relieved against the background of the sky. The sashes were out, and the openings were large. My first intention was to escape through an air-port, but this was abandoned in favor of the more dignified way of making an exit through the passageway leading forward through the superstructure. I groped my way through the cabin into the passage, and along the passage to the outer door. The passage turned to the right, or starboard, near the forward part of the superstructure.

At the turning, some one ran into me violently. I asked who it was. It was Private William Anthony, the orderly at the cabin door. He said

PRIVATE WILLIAM ANTHONY

The Explosion

something apologetic, and reported that the ship had been blown up and was sinking. He was directed to go out on the quarter-deck, and I followed him. Anthony has been pictured as making an exceedingly formal salute on that occasion. The dramatic effect of a salute cannot add to his heroism. If he had made a salute it could not have been seen in the blackness of that compartment. Anthony did his whole duty, at great personal risk, at a time when he might have evaded the danger without question, and deserved all the commendation that he received for his act. He hung near me with unflagging zeal and watchfulness that night until the ship was abandoned.

I stood for a moment on the starboard side of the main-deck, forward of the after-superstructure, looking toward the immense dark mass that loomed up amidships, but could see nothing distinctly. There I remained for a few seconds in an effort to grasp the situation, and then asked Anthony for the exact time. He replied: "The explosion took place at nine-forty, sir." It was soon necessary to retire from the main-deck, for the after-part of the ship was sinking rapidly. I then went up on the poop-deck. By this time Lieutenant-Commander Wainwright and others were near me. Everybody was impressed by

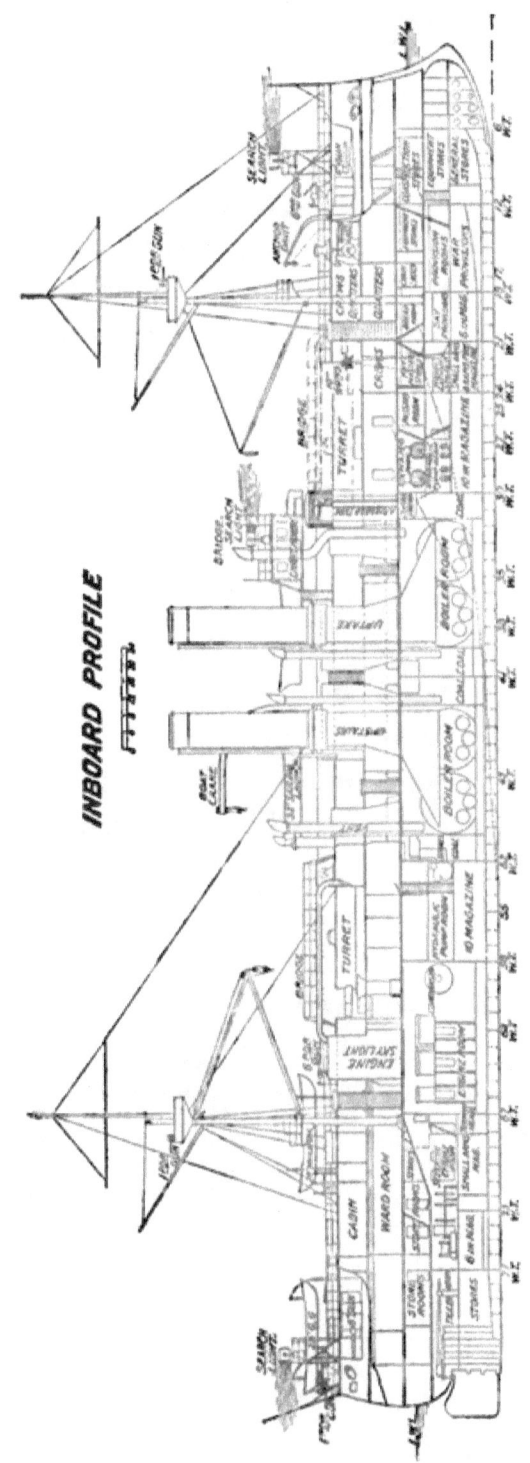

INBOARD PROFILE OF THE "MAINE."

The star near the foremast indicates the height to which some of the keel-plates were blown, and the dotted lines leading down from it the lifting of the keel.

The Explosion

the solemnity of the disaster, but there was no excitement apparent; perfect discipline prevailed.

The question has been asked many times if I believed then that the *Maine* was blown up from the outside. My answer to this has been that my first order on reaching the deck was to post sentries about the ship. I knew that the *Maine* had been blown up, and believed that she had been blown up from the outside. Therefore I ordered a measure which was intended to guard against attack. There was no need for the order, but I am writing of first impressions. There was the sound of many voices from the shore, suggestive of cheers.

I stood on the starboard side-rail of the poop and held on to the main-rigging in order to see over the poop-awning, which was bagged and covered with debris. I was still trying to take in the situation more completely. The officers were near me and showing a courteous recognition of my authority and responsibility. Directions were given in a low tone to Executive Officer Wainwright, who himself gave orders quietly and directed operations. Fire broke out in the mass amidships. Orders were given to flood the forward magazine, but the forward part of the ship was found to be under water. Inquiry as to the after-magazines and the guncotton magazine in the after-part of the ship showed a like condition of those compartments, as reported by those who had escaped from the ward-room and junior officers' quarters. In the captain's spare pantry in the after-superstructure there was spare ammunition. It was seen that this would soon be submerged, and that precautions in respect to the magazines were unnecessary.

The great loss of life was not then fully realized. Our eyes were not yet accustomed to the darkness. Most of us had come from the glare of the electric lights. The flames increased in the central superstructure, and I directed Lieutenant-Commander Wainwright to make an effort to play streams on the fire if practicable. He went forward on the poop-awning, accompanied by Lieutenant Hood and Naval Cadets Boyd and Cluverius, making a gallant inspection in the region of the fire, but was soon obliged to report that nothing could be done. The fire-mains and all other facilities were destroyed, and men were not available for the service.

We then began to realize more clearly the full extent of the damage. One of the smoke-stacks was lying in the water on the starboard side. Although it was almost directly under me, I had not at first identified it. As my eyes became more accustomed to the darkness, I could see,

Mero (Chief Machinist). Brofeldt (Chief Gunner's Mate).

CHIEF MACHINISTS' CABIN. THE FOUR MEN MENTIONED WERE LOST. THE OTHERS WERE NO LONGER ATTACHED TO THE "MAINE."

The Explosion

dimly, white forms on the water, and hear faint cries for help. Realizing that the white forms were our own men, boats were lowered at once and sent to the assistance of the injured and drowning men. Orders were given, but they were hardly necessary: the resourceful intelligence of the officers suggested correct measures in the emergency. Only three of our fifteen boats were available—the barge, the captain's gig, and the whale-boat. The barge was badly injured. Two of these were manned by officers and men jointly. How long they were gone from the ship I cannot recall, but probably fifteen minutes. Those of us who were left on board remained quietly on the poop-deck.

Nothing further could be done; the ship was settling rapidly. There was one wounded man on the poop; he had been hauled from under a ventilator on the main-deck by Lieutenants Hood and Blandin just as the water was rising over him. Other boats, too, were rescuing the wounded and drowning men. Chief among them were the boats from the *Alfonso XII*, and from the steamer *City of Washington*. The visiting boats had arrived promptly, and were unsparing of effort in saving the wounded. The Spanish officers and crews did all that humanity and gallantry could compass. During the absence of our boats the

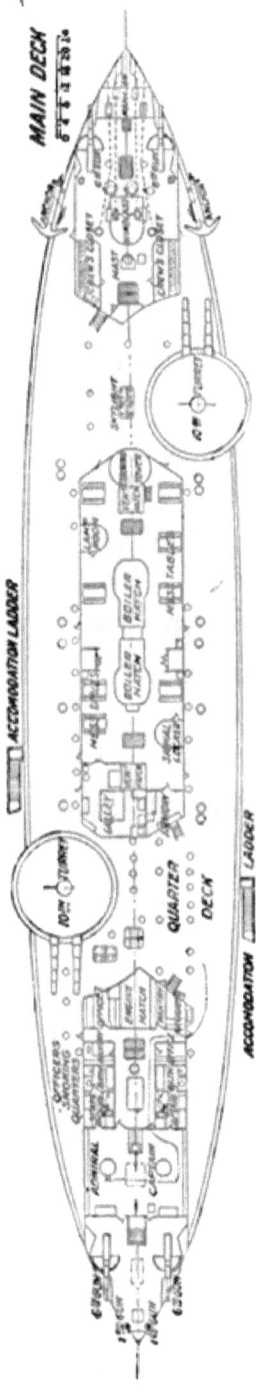

THE MAIN-DECK.

The x in the admiral's cabin shows where Captain Sigsbee was sitting, and the dotted line from it indicates his course in escaping to the quarter-deck.

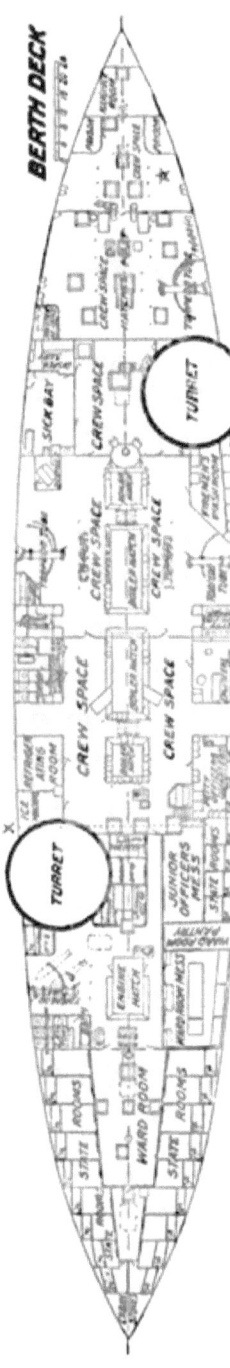

THE BERTH-DECK, ON WHICH MOST OF THE OFFICERS AND CREW WERE QUARTERED. The star indicates where one of the two men saved from the berth-deck was sleeping.

Only two persons escaped from the space between the bow and the x near the after-turret.

The Explosion

fire in the wreck of the central superstructure became fiercer. The spare ammunition that had been stowed in the pilot-house or thrown up from the magazines below was exploding in detail. It continued to explode at intervals until nearly two o'clock in the morning.

At night it was the custom on board the *Maine* to close all water-tight compartments except the few needed to afford passageway for the crew. They had been reported closed as usual that night. Down the cabin skylights the air could be heard whistling through the seams of the doors and hatches, indicating that even the after-bulkheads had been so strained as to admit the water into the compartments. Presently Lieutenant-Commander Wainwright came to me and reported that our boats had returned alongside the ship at the stern, and that all the wounded that could be found had been gathered in and sent to the Spanish cruiser and the *City of Washington* and elsewhere. The after-part of the poop-deck of the *Maine*, the highest intact point above water, was then level with the gig's gunwale, while that boat was in the water alongside. We had done everything that could be done, so far as could be seen.

It was a hard blow to be obliged to leave the *Maine;* none of us desired to leave while any part of her poop remained above water. We waited until satisfied that she was resting on the bottom of the harbor. Lieutenant-Commander Wainwright then whispered to me that he thought the forward ten-inch magazine had been thrown up into the burning material amidships and might explode at any time, with further disastrous effects. He was then directed to get everybody into the boats, which was done. It was an easy operation; one had only to step directly from the deck into the boat. There was still some delay to make sure that the ship's stern had grounded, and still more because of the extreme politeness of the officers, who considerately offered me a steadying hand to step into the boat. Lieutenant-Commander Wainwright stood on one side and Lieutenant Holman on the other; each offered me a hand. I suggested the propriety of my being the last to leave, and requested them to precede me, which they did. There was favorable comment later in the press because I left last. It is a fact that I was the last to leave, which was only proper; that is to say, it would have been improper otherwise; but virtually all left last. The fine conduct of those who came under my observation that night was conspicuous and touching. The heroism of the wounded men I did not see at the time, but after-

THE LAST SCENE ON THE SINKING DECK OF THE "MAINE."

The Explosion

ward good reports of their behavior were very common. The patient way in which they bore themselves left no doubt that they added new honors to the service when the *Maine* went down.

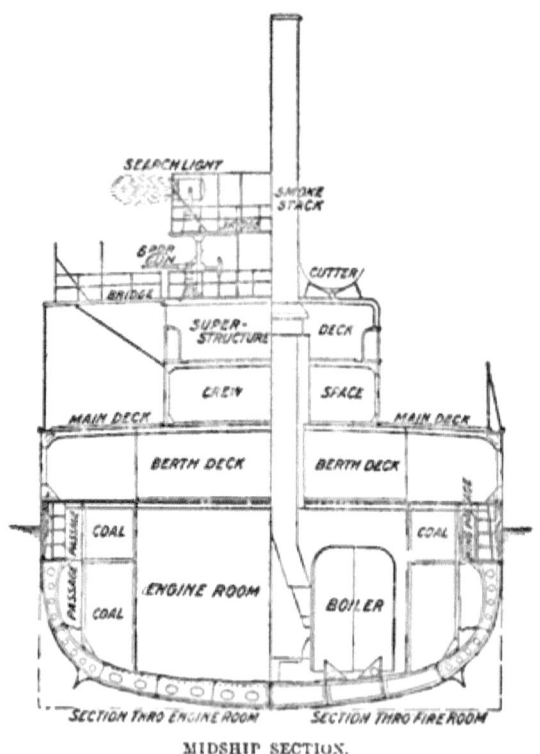

MIDSHIP SECTION.
Only half of the bridge and smoke-stack are shown.

Our boats pulled to the *City of Washington*. On the trip I called, or sent, to the rescuing boats, requesting them to leave the vicinity of the wreck, and informing them that there might be another explosion. Mr. Sylvester Scovel, the newspaper

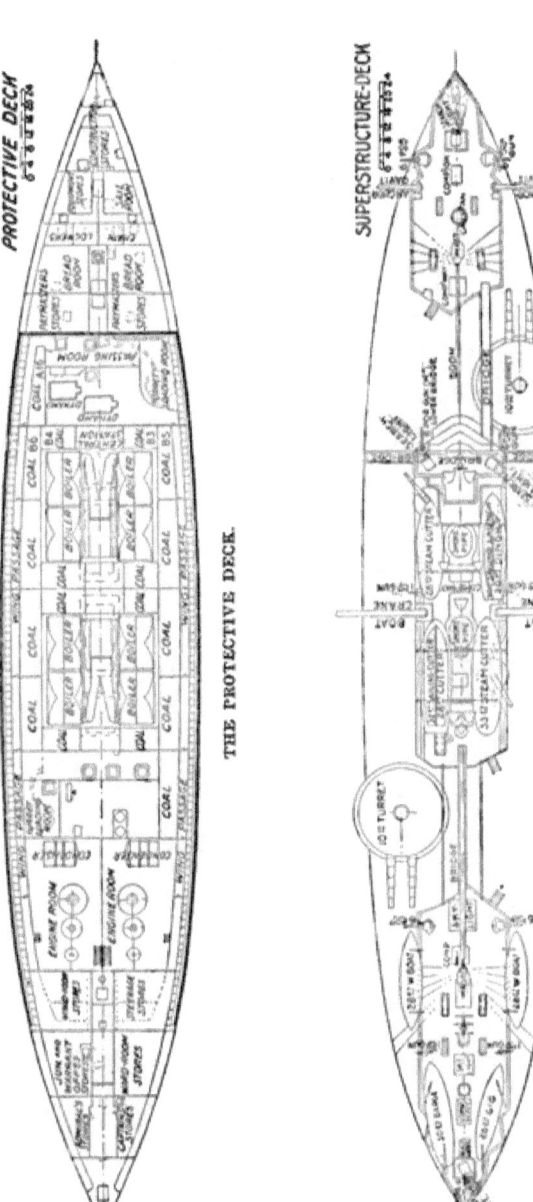

THE PROTECTIVE DECK.

THE SUPERSTRUCTURE-DECK.

The Explosion

correspondent, was asked to translate my request to the Spanish boats, which he did.

On arriving on board the *City of Washington*, I found there a number of our wounded men. They had been carried below into the dining-saloon, where they had been placed on mattresses. They were carefully tended by both officers and crew of the vessel. Every attention that the resources of the vessel admitted had been brought to bear in their favor. The *City of Washington*, then under command of Captain Stevens, did great service. The same was true of the *Alfonso XII*, and, it may be, of the other Spanish vessels also. One or more wounded men were cared for on board the Spanish transport *Colon*.

I walked among the wounded some minutes, and spent a few more in watching the fitful explosion of ammunition on board the *Maine*. Then I went to the captain's cabin, and composed my first telegram to the Navy Department, a facsimile of which faces page 76. I had already directed that a muster be taken of the survivors, and had sent a request to the captain of the *Alfonso XII* that he keep one or more patrol-boats about the wreck. The relations between the United States and Spain had reached a condition of such extreme tension that the patience of the people of the United States was about exhausted. Realizing this fully that night, I feared the result of first impressions of the great disaster on our people, for I found it necessary to repress my own suspicions. I wished them, as a matter of national pride and duty, to take time for consideration. Naval officers, no less than other citizens, have unlimited confidence in the sober judgment of the people of the United States. It seemed also to be a duty of my position to sustain the government during the period of excitement or indignation that was likely to follow the reception of the first report; therefore I took the course of giving to my telegram an uncommonly strong advisory character. The facsimile illustration of the telegram shows that, after advising that public opinion be suspended, and signing my name, I erased the name, and added a few more words relative to the visit and sympathy of the Spanish officers. I added these additional words to strengthen the quieting effect of the telegram. After my name had been signed in the first instance, I was informed that a number of Spanish officers — civil, military, and naval — had arrived on board to express sympathy. I went out on the deck, greeted these gentlemen, and thanked them for their visit. Among them were Dr. Congosto, secre-

New York and Cuba Mail Steamship Company

NEW YORK
TO
HAVANA
MATANZAS, CARDENAS,
SAGUA LA GRANDE,
NASSAU
SANTIAGO DE CUBA
CIENFUEGOS

NEW YORK
TO
VERA CRUZ
PROGRESO
CAMPECHE
FRONTERA
TAMPICO
TUXPAM

JAMES E. WARD & CO., Agents
113 Wall Street.

189_

Secnav —
Washington, D.C.

Maine blown up in Havana harbor at nine forty to night and destroyed. Many wounded and doubtless more killed or drowned. Wounded and others on board Spanish man of war and Ward Line Steamer. ~~Co_____~~ Send Light House Tenders from Key West— ~~_____~~ for crew and the few pieces of equipment above water. None has clothing other than that upon him. Public opinion should be suspended until further report. All officers believed to be saved. Jenkins and Merritt not yet accounted for. ~~Sigsbee~~ ~~Representative of~~ Many Spanish Officers including representative of General Blanco now with me to express sympathy. Sigsbee

FACSIMILE, REDUCED, OF CAPTAIN SIGSBEE'S MESSAGE TO THE SECRETARY OF THE NAVY, "SECNAV" BEING THE TELEGRAPHIC ADDRESS OF THE LATTER.

The Explosion

tary-general of the island; General Salano, chief of staff to General Blanco; the civil governor of the province, and a number of others whose names I cannot now remember. I think the captain of the *Alfonso XII* was also there. After asking them to excuse me for a few moments, to complete my telegram, I returned to the captain's cabin, erased the first signature, and added the additional words. I then called in Dr. Congosto, read the telegram to him, and stated that, as there would be great excitement in the United States, it was my duty to diminish it so far as possible. Dr. Congosto had been a Spanish consul in the United States, and a practising physician there for a number of years. He remarked feelingly that my telegram was "very kind."

The next step was to get the despatch over the cable. It was written about fifteen minutes after we left the *Maine*, and had to be taken ashore in a boat, and thence in a cab to the telegraph office. It must therefore have reached the cable office about eleven o'clock. There was a likelihood that the office would be closed at that time of night, but Dr. Congosto promised me the right of way over the cable, and gave directions that the office, if closed, should be reopened. I requested Mr. George Bronson Rea, then cor-

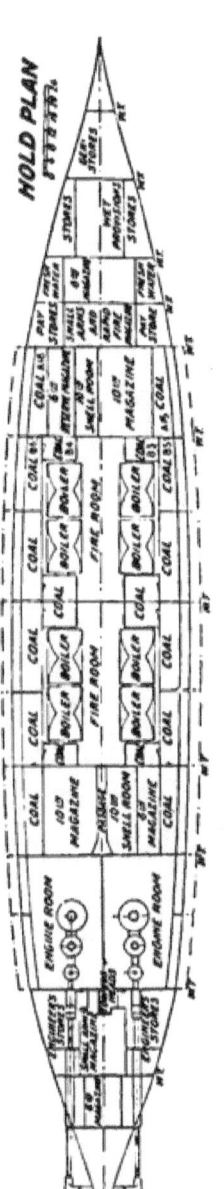

THE HOLD PLAN.

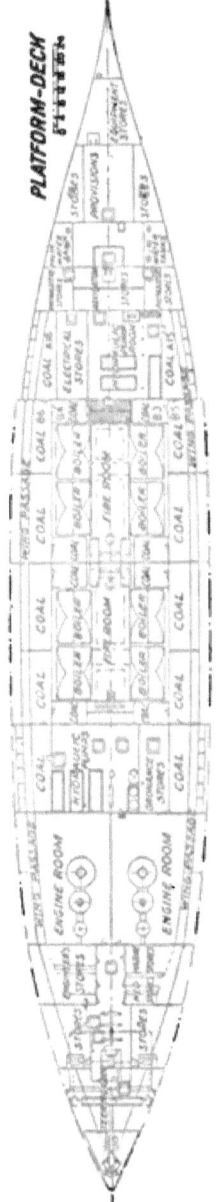

THE PLATFORM-DECK.

The Explosion

respondent, I think, of "Harper's Weekly," to carry the telegram ashore and send it. He readily consented. At the same time he also sent for me a telegram to Commander Forsyth, commandant of the naval station at Key West, conveying information of the disaster to Admiral Sicard. At the office he transcribed them to the regular forms; then, it appears, he sent the original of the longer despatch to a New York newspaper, where it was reproduced. Mr. Rea soon afterward volunteered to return me the original of the latter. It is through his courtesy that it is now in my possession. At the time it was written it did not occur to me that the document would be deemed worthy of preservation. It has been said in criticism that I should have used the word "judgment" instead of "opinion" in framing my telegram. "Opinion" was the more diplomatic word under the circumstances. The other might have given rise to a contention with the censor. It will be shown later how censorship in Cuba was applied to an official despatch from me to Washington announcing the grounding of my vessel by a Spanish pilot.

Having disposed of the telegram, I returned to the Spanish officials. They seemed especially desirous of having my opinion as to the cause of the explosion. I invariably answered that I

The "Maine"

must await investigation. General Salano, a handsome and distinguished-looking officer, of dignified bearing and address, declared to me that the Spanish authorities knew nothing whatever as to the cause of the destruction of the *Maine*. He said that he made the assertion as a man, an officer, and a Spaniard. I assured him of my ready acceptance of his statement, and remarked that I had not yet permitted myself to give any thought to the question of responsibility for the disaster. The Spanish officers remained only a short time. In the length of their visit, and the character of it, they showed exquisite tact. General Fitzhugh Lee arrived on board the *City of Washington* soon after we boarded her, and remained all night, I think. It has always seemed to me that it took high courage for the United States consul-general to traverse the city and the water during the uncertainties of those early hours.

After the first muster that night it was reported to me that only eighty-four or eighty-five survivors could be found. Recent summary (see Crew List and Mortuary Statistics, Appendices G and H) shows that only sixteen of the crew were wholly unhurt. Two officers and two hundred and fifty men were killed. One hundred and two people were saved, but later eight of these died

Forward Key West —

Rear Admiral Sampson Wishes to
report sent of from Montauk to
Jamaica, many killed and wounded
300 land crew vessels of all arms sink
all.

Sigsbee

The Explosion

at Havana. Some of the wounded were taken to the landing at the Machina, where they were cared for by the fire organizations of Havana. The wounded who were gathered in by the Spaniards and Americans that night were sent to two hospitals in Havana, the Alfonso XIII and the San Ambrosio. I was inclined to feel offended when the commanding officer of the cruiser *Alfonso XII* did not refer to me before he sent the wounded ashore; but I soon came to the conclusion that he had used his best judgment, and with every desire to be kind and sympathetic. The subsequent treatment of our wounded by the Spaniards was most considerate and humane. They did all that they habitually did for their own people, and even more.

This paper was given the form of a personal experience, first, because I alone was personally connected with the complete chain of incidents to be recited; secondly, because the form promised less labor of preparation in the time at my disposal. But the explosion, and its immediate consequences, were too momentous and harrowing, and too varied, to be narrowed down to the view of one person, even in so personal a narrative. None can ever know the awful scenes of consternation, despair, and suffering down in the forward compartments of the stricken ship; of men wounded, or drowning in the swirl of water, or confined in a closed compartment gradually filling with water. But from those so favorably situated that escape was possible, much may be gathered to enable us to form a conception of the general chaos. It is comforting to believe that most of those who were lost were killed instantly; and it is probably true, also, for many of the wounded who recovered had no knowledge of the explosion; they remembered no sensations, except that they awoke and found themselves wounded and in a strange place.

The phenomena of the explosion, as witnessed by different persons, and the personal experiences of officers and men, may be derived from the "Report of the Naval Court of Inquiry upon the Destruction of the United States Battle-ship *Maine*."[1] I have, in addition, reports from the officers of the *Maine*, and my recollections of conversations with those who were informed in various directions.

Before the court, Captain Frederick G. Teasdale, master of the British bark *Deva*, testified as follows: He was aboard the *Deva*, which was lying at a wharf at Regla, from a quarter to half a mile from the *Maine*. He said, in continua-

[1] United States Senate Document No. 207, Fifty-fifth Congress, Second Session.

The Explosion

tion of his previous testimony: ". . . sitting at the cabin table writing when I heard the explosion. I thought the ship had been collided with. I ran on deck when I heard the explosion. I felt a very severe shock in my head, also. I seized my head this way [indicating]. I thought I was shot, or something. The transoms of the doors of the cabin are fitted in the studs on the side, and they were knocked out of place with the shock. The first seemed to be a shot, and then a second, or probably two seconds, after the first report that I heard, I heard a tremendous explosion; but as soon as I heard the first report,—it was a very small one,— thinking something had happened to the ship, I rushed on deck, and was on deck just in time to see the whole debris going up in the air. . . . The stuff ascended, I should say, one hundred and fifty or one hundred and sixty feet up in the air. It seemed to go comparatively straight until it reached its highest point of ascent; then it divided and passed off in kinds of rolls or clouds. Then I saw a series of lights flying from it again. Some of them were lights — incandescent lights. Sometimes they appeared to be brighter, and sometimes they appeared to be dim, as they passed through the smoke, I should presume. The color of the smoke, I should say, was a very dark slate-color. There were fifteen to twenty of those lights that looked like incandescent lights. The smoke did not seem to be black, as you would imagine from an explosion like that. It seemed to be more a slate-color. . . . Quantities of paper and small fragments fell over our ship, and for some time after."

Mr. Sigmund Rothschild, a passenger on board the *City of Washington*, went on deck about half-past nine with his fellow-passenger Mr. Wertheimer. They drew chairs toward the railing. Mr. Rothschild testified: "In doing so, I had brought my chair just about in this condition [indicating], and had not sat down when I heard a shot, the noise of a shot. I looked around, and I saw the bow of the *Maine* rise a little, go a little out of the water. It could n't have been more than a few seconds after that noise, that shot, that there came in the center of the ship a terrible mass of fire and explosion, and everything went over our heads, a black mass. We could not tell what it was. It was all black. Then we heard a noise of falling material on the place where we had been right near the smoking-room. One of the life-boats, which was hanging, had a piece go through it and made a big hole in it. After we saw that mass go up, the whole boat [*Maine*] lifted out, I should

VIEW OF THE WRECK FROM THE STERN.

judge, about two feet. As she lifted out, the bow went right down.... We stood spellbound, and cried to the captain [of the *City of Washington*]. The captain gave orders to lower the boats, and two of the boats, which were partly lowered, were found broken through with big holes. Some iron pieces had fallen through them. Naturally, that made a delay, and they had to run for the other boats, or else we would have been a few minutes sooner in the water. Then the stern stood out like this, in this direction [indicating], and there was a cry from the people: 'Help!' and 'Lord God, help us!' and 'Help! Help!' The noise of the cry from the mass of human voices in the boat [*Maine*] did not last but a minute or two. When the ship was going down, there was the cry of a mass of people, but that was a murmur. That was not so loud as the single voices which were in the water. That did not last but a minute, and by that time we saw somebody on the deck in the stern of the ship, and it took about a few minutes when the boats commenced to bring in the officers. [The last to come on board.] We took them to our rooms. A great many of them came without anything on but a pair of pants and nothing else. That is about the whole story in regard to the shot." Mr. Louis Wertheimer, another passenger aboard the *City of Washington*, gave testimony to the same effect.

In his testimony First Officer George Cornell of the *City of Washington* said: "I was standing on the gangway, and giving the quartermaster orders to call the men at five o'clock in the morning. While I was standing there I heard a rumbling sound, and we saw the *Maine* raise up forward. After that the explosion occurred, and the stuff was flying in the air in all directions. She sank immediately at the forward end."

Captain Frank Stevens, master of the *City of Washington*, testified: "I heard a dull, muffled explosion and commotion, like as though it was under the water, followed instantly by a terrific explosion, lighting up the air with a dull red glare, filling the air full of flying missiles, which lit all around us. We were struck, I think, in four places."

It has been said before that some of the *Maine's* officers and some of the crew were on the main or upper deck at the time of the explosion. We have the testimony of some of them relative to the phenomena. Lieutenant John Hood was one of these. His testimony is very interesting. I quote it at some length: "I was sitting on the port side of the deck, with my feet

The Explosion

on the rail, and I both heard and felt — felt more than I heard — a big explosion, that sounded and felt like an under-water explosion. I was under the impression that it came from forward, starboard, at the time. I instantly turned my head, and the instant I turned my head there was a second explosion. I saw the whole starboard side of the deck, and everything above it as far aft as the after-end of the superstructure, spring up in the air, with all kinds of objects in it — a regular crater-like performance, with flames and everything else coming up. I immediately sprang myself behind the edge of the superstructure, as there were a number of objects flying in my direction, for shelter. I ran very quickly aft, as fast as I could, along the after-end of the superstructure, and climbed up on a kind of step. I went under the barge, and by the time I went up on the superstructure this explosion had passed. The objects had stopped flying around. Then I saw on the starboard side there was an immense mass of foaming water and wreckage and groaning men out there. It was scattered around in a circle, I should say about a hundred yards in diameter, off on the starboard side. I immediately proceeded to lower the gig, with the help of another man. After I got that in the water several officers jumped in it, and one or two men. In the meantime somebody else was lowering the other boat on the port side. I heard some groans forward, and ran forward on the quarter-deck down the poop-ladder, and I immediately brought up on an immense pile of wreckage. I saw one man there, who had been thrown from somewhere, pinned down by a ventilator."

THE COURT. "May I interrupt Mr. Hood a moment? He said several officers jumped into the gig. He does not say for what purpose or what they did. That might leave a bad impression unless he states what the object was."

ANSWER. "They jumped into the gig, commanded to pick up these wounded men whom we heard out in the water. The orders had been given by the captain and the executive officer to lower the boats as soon as they came on deck. I spoke of lowering the gig because I was on the deck before they got up there, and began to lower it anyway, to pick up these men. As I was saying a minute ago, I found this one man lying there on the quarter-deck in this wreckage, pinned down by a ventilator. With Mr. Blandin's help we got him up just in time before the water rose over him. The captain and the executive officer ordered the magazines to be closed

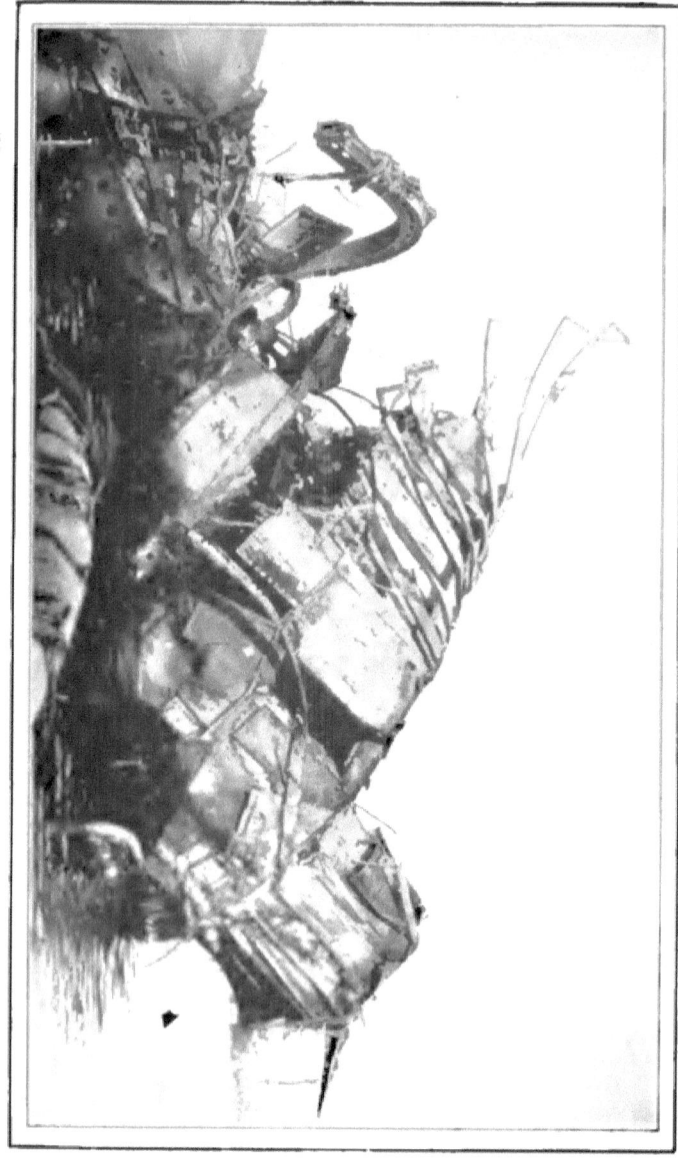

THE CENTRAL SUPERSTRUCTURE, INCLUDING THE CONNING TOWER, THROWN UPSIDE DOWN.

The Explosion

[flooded]. We all saw at once that it would be no use flooding the magazines. We saw that the magazines were flooding themselves. Then the captain said he wanted the fire put out that was starting up in the wreckage. I made my way forward through the wreck and debris, up to the middle superstructure, to see if anything could be done toward putting out this fire. When I got there I found nothing could be done, because the whole thing was gone.

"When I climbed up on this wreck on the superstructure I saw similar piles of wreckage on the port side which I had not seen before, and I saw some men struggling in that, in the water; but there were half a dozen boats there, I suppose, picking them up and hauling them out; and after pulling down some burning swings and things that were starting to burn aft, to stop any fire from catching aft, I came aft again out of the wreckage. There was no living thing up there at that time. Shortly after that we all left the ship. There were two distinct explosions,— big ones,— and they were followed by a number of smaller explosions, which I took at once to be what they were, I suppose — explosions of separate charges of the blown-up magazine. The instant this first explosion occurred I knew the ship was gone completely, and the second explosion only assisted her to go a little quicker. She began to go down instantly. The interval between the two was so short that I only had time to turn my head and see the second. She sank on the forward end — went down like a shot. In the short time that I took to run the length of that short superstructure aft, the deck canted down, showing that her bow had gone at once.

"At the same time the ship heeled over considerably to port, I should say about ten degrees, the highest amount, and then the stern began to sink very rapidly, too; so rapidly that by the time I got that gig lowered, with the assistance of another man or two, the upper quarter-deck was under water, and the stern was sinking so quickly that when I began to pick this man up, whom I spoke of on the quarter-deck, the deck was still out of water. Before I got this ventilator off him — it did n't take very long, as Mr. Blandin assisted to move that to get him up — the water was over my knees, and just catching this fellow's head, the stern was sinking that quickly. The bow had gone down, as I say, instantly."

Special interest attaches to the personal experiences of Lieutenant John H. Blandin, who has since died. The disaster appeared to affect him greatly, and led, doubtless, to the impairment

The Explosion

of his health. He had made an unusually long tour of continuous sea duty, and had suffered considerable disappointment because of his failure to secure his detachment from the *Maine*. For certain public reasons it had not been granted him, but it would have come soon. He said: "After the third quarter-watch at nine o'clock was piped down, I was on the starboard side of the deck, walking up and down. I looked over the side, and then went over to the port side and took a look. I don't remember seeing any boats at all in sight. I thought at the time the harbor was very free from boats. I thought it was about three bells, and I walked over to the port side of the deck, just abaft the after-turret. Mr. Hood came up shortly afterward, and was talking to me when the explosion occurred. I am under the impression that there were two explosions, though I could not be sure of it. Mr. Hood started aft to get on the poop to lower the boats, I suppose, and I followed him. Something struck me on the head. My cap was in my hand. My head was slightly cut, and I was partially knocked over, but not stunned. I climbed on the poop and went on the starboard side, and found Captain Sigsbee there. I reported to him. He ordered the boats lowered at once to pick up any of the wounded. The officers very rapidly got on the poop, and there were one or two men there, but very few.

"The barge and gig were lowered, and just then I heard a man crying out down on the quarter-deck. I went to the ladder, and I saw Mr. Hood trying to pull a ventilator off the man's legs. He was lying in the wreckage, jammed there. The water then was not deep. I went down and helped Mr. Hood to pull this ventilator off, and carried the man on the poop, with the help of Private Loftus, I think it was. It was a private man [marine]. Then the captain told Mr. Wainwright to see if anything could be done to put out the fire. Mr. Wainwright went forward to the middle superstructure, and shortly afterward came back and reported to the captain that it was hopeless to try to do anything. Then in a very few moments the captain decided that it was hopeless, and gave the order to abandon ship. Boats came from the *Alfonso Doce*, and two boats from the *City of Washington*, and those, with our boats, picked up the wounded and sent most of them, by the captain's order, to the *Alfonso*. There were thirty-four sent there. We abandoned ship, the captain getting in his gig after everybody had left, and went to the *City of Washington*."

One of the narrowest escapes of an officer was

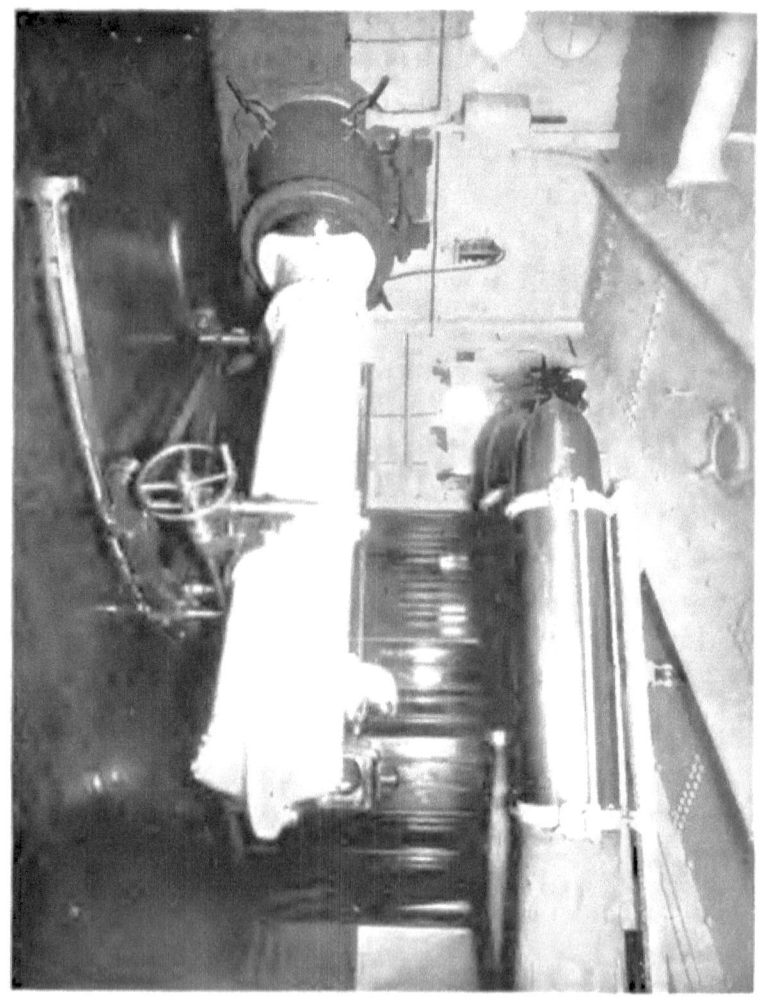

THE AFTER TORPEDO-TUBE (SEE PLAN OF THE BERTH-DECK, PAGE 70, AND TORPEDO-ROOM NEAR THE AFTER-TURRET).

The Explosion

that of Naval Cadet D. F. Boyd, Jr. I quote a large part of his report to me. It gives all that is known of the case of Assistant Engineer Darwin R. Merritt, who was drowned. "About nine-thirty, as well as I am able to judge, on the night of February 15, Assistant Engineer D. R. Merritt and I were sitting in the steerage [junior officers' mess-room] reading, when I heard a dull report, followed by the crashing of splinters and falling of the electric-light fixtures overhead. The lights were extinguished at the first report. I was struck by a small splinter and dazed for a moment. I grasped Mr. Merritt by the arm, exclaiming: 'Out of this! Up on deck!' Together we groped our way out of the steerage, and along the bulkhead in the after torpedo-room, where we met a cloud of steam and tremendous rush of water. The force of the water separated us, and as I was lifted off my feet, I caught a steam-heater pipe, and reached for the steerage-ladder. It was gone. I worked my way along the steam-pipe until I reached the port side of the ship. Water was rushing through the air-port, and as I reached the side, I heard some one cry: 'God help me! God help me!' I think it must have been Merritt. At that moment I found the two torpedoes that were triced up under the deck-beams, and twining my legs

The "Maine"

around them, I worked my way inboard.[1] The water was then at a level of about one foot from the deck-beams. At that moment some burning cellulose flared up, and I was able to reach the hatch-coaming and work my way up on deck. I rushed on the poop, and there found Captain Sigsbee, Lieutenant-Commander Wainwright, Lieutenants Holman and Hood, and Naval Cadet Cluverius. The remaining boats were away, picking up these men in the water. Lieutenant-Commander Wainwright and I then went on the quarter-deck awning and on the middle superstructure to help out any wounded.

"When the captain gave the order to abandon ship, we were brought over in the Ward line steamer *City of Washington's* boat. The boats present, as well as I remember, were two of our boats, two from the *City of Washington*, three from the *Alfonso XII*, and several shore boats."

The circumstances connected with the loss of Lieutenant Friend W. Jenkins have been involved in much mystery. Lieutenant Holman testified that he himself, together with Lieutenants Jungen and Jenkins and Chief Engineer

---

[1] The ladders and hatches by which the officers and others escaped were inboard from this tube. Naval Cadet Boyd clasped his legs around the torpedoes slung to the ceiling, or underside of the main-deck, when the compartment was nearly full of water, and worked his way to the hatch.

Lieutenant Jenkins's body was found wedged against these torpedoes.

The Explosion

Howell, were in the officers' mess-room. All were saved but Lieutenant Jenkins. Mess-attendant John H. Turpin (colored) was in the ward-room pantry, which is next forward of the officers' mess-room. In his testimony Turpin says: "It was a jarring explosion — just one solid explosion, and the ship heaved and lifted like that, and then all was dark. I met Mr. Jenkins in the mess-room, and by that time the water was up to my waist, and the water was running aft. It was all dark in there, and he hollered to me, and he says: 'Which way?' I don't know what he meant by that. I says: 'I don't know which way.' He hollered again: 'Which way?' I says: 'I don't know, sir, which way.' And he hollered the last time; he says: 'Which way?' I says: 'I don't know, sir.' Then I was groping my way, and the water was up to my breast. Mr. Jenkins started forward, and then the whole compartment lit right up. That whole compartment where the torpedoes were lit right up, and I seen Mr. Jenkins then throw up both hands and fall, right by the steerage pantry. Then I groped my way aft, and got to the captain's ladder — the ladder coming out of the ward-room — just as you come out of the ward-room to go up in the cabin. When I got there the ladder was carried away, and somehow or other the man-rope kept fast upon the deck, but the ladder got adrift from it down below in the water. By that time the water was right up even with my chin. Then I commenced to get scared, and in fooling around it happened that a rope touched my arm, and I commenced to climb overhand and got on deck."

Fireman William Gartrell was in the steering-engine room, two decks lower than the officers' mess-room. He was lower down in the ship than any other man that escaped. To reach the level of the officers' mess-rooms he had to run forward about twenty feet, pass through a doorway, spring across to a ladder, climb up two flights of ladders, and pass through another doorway — a narrow and difficult route under the best of conditions (see profile of the *Maine*). I quote his testimony in part: "I could see through the door, sir. It was a kind of a blue flame, and it came all at once. The two of us jumped up, and I went on the port side up the engine-room ladder, and Frank Gardiner he went up the starboard side — at least, he did n't go up, because he hollered to me. He struck the door right there where the partition separates the two doors, and he must have struck his head. He hollered to me; he says: 'O Jesus, Billy, I am gone.' I did n't stop then, because the water

LIEUTENANT FRIEND W. JENKINS
WHO WAS LOST

ASSISTANT ENGINEER DARWIN R. MERRITT
WHO WAS LOST

The Explosion

was up to my knees. I made a break as quick as I could up the ladder, and when I got up the ladder into the steerage-room the ladder was gone. Everything was dark. I could n't see nothing; everything was pitch-dark, and I gave up, or I started to give up. There was a colored fellow with me; I did n't know his name until afterward. His name was Harris. We got hold of each other. I says: 'Let's give up; there is no hope.' I started in to say a prayer the best I knew how, and I heard a voice. It must have been an officer; it could n't have been a man's voice, because he says: 'There is hope, men.' I knew from that that he was an officer. After that I seen a little light. It looked like an awful distance from me, but I made for that light, and when I got there it seemed like I could see the heavens. I got jammed in the ladder. My head was right up against the deck. I seen the ladder, and I caught hold of Harris, and the two of us hugged each other. . . . The ladder was hung crossways on top. There was n't no ladder that we could walk up. The ladder was up above us. . . . I don't know whether I got out first, or this colored fellow, but when I did get out I tried to say a prayer. I looked where I was, and I saw the heavens and everything, and I tried to say a prayer or something, and I fainted away. I felt some one picking me up, and they throwed me overboard."

The foregoing extracts refer to those who escaped from that part of the ship that was not destroyed. The fearful loss of life was forward. I believe only two men escaped from the berth-deck forward of the officers' quarters, the principal sleeping-quarters of the crew, namely, Charles Bergman, boatswain's mate, and Jeremiah Shea, coal-passer. I regret that I have no report of Shea's experience. He was sleeping below the great pile of wreckage that is the most prominent feature in the pictures of the wreck. Afterward, when asked to account for his miraculous escape, he replied: "I think I must be an armor-piercing projectile, sir." Bergman was turned in, in his hammock, which was swung from the beams in the forward crew-space, just abaft the "brig," or prison, on the starboard side. In his testimony Bergman says:

"I heard a terrible crash, an explosion I suppose that was. Something fell, and then after that I got thrown somewhere in a hot place. Wherever that was I don't know. I got burned on my legs and arms, and got my mouth full of ashes and one thing and another. Then the next thing I was in the water — away under the water somewhere, with a lot of wreckage on top

The Explosion

of me that was sinking me down. After I got clear of that I started to come up to the surface of the water again, and I got afoul of some other wreckage. I got my head jammed in, and I could n't get loose, so I let myself go down. Then it carried me down farther. I suppose when it touched the bottom somewhere it sort of opened out a bit, and I got my head out and started for the surface of the water again. I hit a lot of other stuff with my head, and then I got my head above the water. I got picked up by a Spanish boat, one of these shore boats, I think."

The narratives of others might be continued at much greater length, but the advisability is lessened by the existence of a very complete record in the report of the court of inquiry.

At 2 A. M. on the night of the explosion I lay down in a state-room of the *City of Washington*, hoping to get enough sleep to give me a clear head for the difficulties of the following day, which I knew would be great. The bunk was uncomfortable, the weather hot, and the stench from the harbor water disagreeable. A few feet from my state-room the wounded lay. Some of them groaned pitifully, and doubtless unconsciously; one had nausea. I tried hard to ignore all disturbances, but got very little sleep that night.

At daylight I again went among the wounded

men. As I patted a wounded Japanese messman on the shoulder, the poor fellow looked greatly pleased, and made a futile effort to rise up and be respectful. Then I gazed long and sadly at the wreck of the *Maine*. How great the destruction! She had settled in the mud, and her poop-deck, where we had stood at the last moment, was under water. There was no part of her hull visible except that torn and misshapen mass amidships and three pieces of steel jutting out of the water farther forward, one of which was from the bottom plating of the ship. The forward part of the central superstructure had been blown upward and somewhat to starboard, and had folded back on its after-part, carrying the bridge, pilot-house, and six-inch gun and conning-tower with it, and completely capsizing them. The broad surface that was uppermost was the ceiling of the berth-deck, where many men had swung from beam to beam in their hammocks the night before. On the white paint of the ceiling was the impression of two human bodies,— mere dust,— so I was told afterward. The great pile was so torn, twisted, and confused with structural details that the identification of visible parts was only possible after careful study. The foremast had toppled over forward and disappeared. Only one end of the fore signal-yard

VIEW MADE SEVERAL DAYS AFTER THE EXPLOSION.

The Explosion

was above water; this was well forward of everything else, and looked like a spar-buoy. Even the mooring-buoy had gone down. The cellulose from the coffer-dams was still burning.

The *Alfonso XII* and the *City of Washington* had shifted their berths farther from the wreck during the night, to avoid the bursting rapid-fire ammunition. The Spanish patrol-boats were on duty. But saddest of all was the reflection that many dead were down there in the wreck, and that many homes were made desolate. It was not difficult to conceive what the day and the water would bring forth. My thoughts naturally turned toward Jenkins and Merritt, whose safety was in doubt; we had not wholly given them up for lost. Inquiries were made as to their movements the night before, but no hope could be built up.

The officers of the *Maine* were in good physical condition that morning: none showed signs of nervous shock. The same is true of the uninjured men. None had saved more than he had upon him when the explosion came, and some had been wet by the filthy harbor water; kind-hearted passengers and officers of the vessel had supplied deficiencies so far as possible, but we were a gruesome party. During the day the United States despatch-steamer *Fern*, Lieutenant-Commander W. C. Cowles commanding, arrived. So did the steamer *Mangrove* of the United States Lighthouse Establishment, with Commander Samuel Belden, U. S. N., on board, and the American passenger-steamer *Olivette* of the Plant line. Assistant Surgeon Spear of the flagship *New York* and Surgeon Clendenin of the army post at Key West came to render assistance.

 The day after the explosion of the *Maine*, I sent to Key West, by the *Olivette*, every officer and man that could be spared or who could travel. My desire was to retain no one in Havana that could get away; and thereafter the wounded men were taken from the hospitals and sent to Key West as soon as they could bear the journey. Miss Clara Barton, in behalf of the Red Cross Society, offered to place a specially prepared hospital at my service for the wounded men. The offer was gratefully declined on the ground that any removal at all should be to Key West. I retained on duty in Havana Lieutenant-Commander Wainwright, Paymaster Ray, Dr. Heneberger, Chaplain Chidwick, Lieutenant Holman, and Naval Cadets Holden and Cluverius. I also retained my orderly, Private William Anthony, and a very worthy gunner's mate named Bullock. The greater part of that day was spent on the water, on board the visiting vessels already named, receiving reports, parting

The Explosion

with the officers and men, and preparing for the work to come. In the forenoon I sent the following telegram to the Secretary of the Navy:

> Advise sending wrecking-vessel at once. *Maine* submerged except debris. Mostly work for divers now. Jenkins and Merritt still missing. Little hope for their safety. Those known to be saved are: officers, 24; uninjured, crew, 18; wounded now on Ward line steamer, in city hospitals and hotels, 59, so far as known. All others went down on board or near the *Maine*. Total lost or missing, 253. With several exceptions, no officer or man has more than a part of a suit of clothing, and that is wet with water. Ward steamer leaves for Mexico at 2 this afternoon. The officers saved are uninjured. Damage was in compartments of crew. Am preparing to telegraph list of saved and wounded. *Olivette* leaves for Key West at 1 P. M. Will send by her to Key West officers saved, except myself and Wainwright, Holman, Heneberger, Ray, and Holden. Will turn over three uninjured boats to captain of port, with request for safe-keeping. Will send all wounded men to hospital in Havana.

The following telegram was received from the Secretary:

> The President directs me to express for himself and the people of the United States his profound sympathy with the officers and crew of the *Maine*, and desires that no expense be spared in providing for the survivors and caring for the dead.

The *Olivette* and the *City of Washington* left during the afternoon, the latter for Vera Cruz, Mexico, the wounded men having been transferred from her to the San Ambrosio Hospital.

The "Maine"

At 4 P. M. I went ashore and took up my quarters at the Hotel Inglaterra, where General Lee lived. Others of the *Maine's* officers were there with me or at another hotel near by. Lieutenant-Commander Wainwright preferred to remain on board the *Fern* with his friend, Lieutenant-Commander Cowles. Anthony and Bullock went with me to the Inglaterra. This hotel occupies a central position with respect to the harbor, the palace, the cable office, the consulate, the morgue, and the cemetery. It was the rational residence for me at the time. I remained there about a week. There were many evidences that the people of Havana, as a body, gave us sincere sympathy, at least at that time. That day, General Lee, whose opportunity for judging was better than mine, sent the following telegram to the Department of State:

Profound sorrow expressed by government and municipal authorities, consuls of foreign nations, organized bodies of all sorts, and citizens generally. Flags at half-mast on governor-general's palace, on shipping in harbor, and in city. Business suspended; theaters closed. Dead number about 260. Officers' quarters being in rear and seamen's forward, where explosion took place, accounts for greater proportional loss of sailors. Funeral to-morrow at 3 P. M. Officers Jenkins and Merritt still missing. Suppose you ask that naval court of inquiry be held to ascertain cause of explosion. Hope our people will repress excitement and calmly await decision.

BOTTOM-PLATING, PROTECTIVE DECK, AND SECOND LONGITUDINAL SHOWING ABOVE THE WATER.

The Explosion

The swirl of responsibilities in which I found myself can well be understood. I had lost my vessel and more than two hundred and fifty of my crew in a foreign port, politically unfriendly at least, where I could not command the resources that were needed. It was a land of one creed. The recovery of the dead was reported to me hour after hour; more were down in the wreck. State papers must be recovered, the vessel protected, the dead assembled, coffined, and buried. Bereaved families and friends would be emotional, and might not be satisfied with my measures. There were questions of diplomacy, policy, investigation, resources, and expense; there were telegrams, private and official, to answer and to frame, during the day and far into the night, and statistics to gather and report. The situation was complex and trying. Although without personal dread of the responsibility as relating to myself or my career, I was much concerned to do only that which would meet the approval of my own government and of the relatives of the deceased men of the *Maine*.

We were face to face with innumerable difficulties when a large measure of relief came from an unexpected source. That night General Blanco, accompanied by the mayor of Havana, visited me at the hotel, where they personally

The "Maine"

expressed their sympathy and made offers of service. They requested that the authorities of Havana be allowed to give public burial to the dead already recovered from the *Maine*, in order that public sympathy and sorrow might be shown, and honor done the dead. While it seemed probable that the acceptance of this offer would not meet with approval on all sides among Americans who were most concerned, it was accepted with suitable acknowledgments. General Lee thought as I did in the matter. It is gratifying to remember that we were always in harmony. Relative to the visit of General Blanco and the mayor of Havana, I sent the following telegram to the Secretary of the Navy:

> General Blanco called on me personally at the hotel last night, and also the mayor of the city. They have requested me to permit the government here to give a public burial to the dead already found, in order that public sympathy may be expressed thereby, and due honor shown the dead. Ground for the burial has been secured. It is assumed that I am expected by the department to bury the dead here. In fact, it would be impracticable to transport remains to the United States. Means and facilities are lacking. I have accepted the offer of the authorities, and there will be a public funeral at 3 o'clock to-day. All here from the *Maine* will go; also a delegation from the *Fern*. Fifteen bodies recovered during operations. [Further] operations prevented by rough weather.

On the afternoon of February 17, funeral services were held over nineteen bodies, the first that were recovered. It was only necessary for the officers of the *Maine* to attend the funeral as mourners for the dead. We were notified that we were to appear at three o'clock at the municipal palace, which forms part of the building in which the government of the island is quartered, and in which the captain-general has his residence. On entering one of the state apartments, we found nineteen coffins, covered with mourning emblems of various kinds and from all classes of people, bearing the names of individuals and organizations — civic, military, and naval. No greater demonstration of sympathy could have been made.

At the gathering in the municipal palace I conversed with Dr. Congosto, and asked him to present me to the Bishop of Havana. Appreciating the sentiments of the relatives of those who were lost, I had previously asked Chaplain Chidwick if some arrangement could not be made whereby prayers might be read over the Protestant dead by a Protestant clergyman or by myself. He had referred the question to the bishop, who had politely negatived the proposition. I did not like this, because I desired to do everything in my power to comfort the families and friends of the deceased men; therefore, when I was presented to the bishop, I renewed my request, with a statement of the difficulties of the case. The bishop was very kind, but had to regret his inability to concede the point. I was much disturbed; in fact, I was indignant, for my mood in the presence of those coffins was one requiring great effort at self-repression; therefore I remarked to Dr. Congosto that if I had been fully prepared for a refusal I should probably not have felt free to accept the offer of the Spanish authorities to take charge of the funeral ceremonies — that I should have preferred to take them under my own charge, in such a way that I could have given to each creed freedom to bury its dead after its own forms. In this I was doubtless lacking in tact. Nevertheless I was sincere. My position, sentimentally, was so difficult that I felt that I could speak plainly to Dr. Congosto, who, as I have already said, had lived in the United States. In my opinion, the Bishop of Havana and Chaplain Chidwick were quite acceptable to officiate at the grave of any Christian: but this was not a matter for my opinion alone; others were to be considered. Having failed in my second request, I next requested that Chaplain Chidwick might officiate at the grave. This was promptly granted. I had brought to the palace an Episcopal prayer-book, which I had procured at the last minute, intending to read the service myself, for no Prot-

FUNERAL OF NINETEEN OF THE "MAINE'S" DEAD, FROM THE MUNICIPAL PALACE, HAVANA.

The Explosion

estant clergyman could be found in Havana; and, in fact, I did read the service, a part at a time, as opportunity offered, chiefly in the carriage on the way to the cemetery, and afterward in my room at the hotel.

The funeral cortège was very imposing. In addition to the hearses, there were many carriages and also a large military, naval, and civic escort, provided by the Spaniards. Even the poor reconcentrados were in line. No such demonstration had been made in Havana for very many years; in fact, I was informed that it had not been paralleled, except in one instance, in the history of Havana. The Bishop of Havana went to the cemetery in person, which, I was also informed, was a most unusual mark of sympathy. As the procession passed through the streets it seemed that all the people of Havana were present along the route, in respectful sympathy. At a certain point the carriages were stopped; the occupants alighted and marched, as an additional act of respect, for some distance, when they again entered the carriages and proceeded therein through the suburbs to the Colon Cemetery, one of the most beautiful that I have ever seen. The carriages were left just within the entrance, and the procession continued to the grave on foot.

The "Maine"

After the burial I again presented myself to the bishop, and apologized for having made a request which could not meet his approval. I thanked him for his sympathy and kindness, and assured him that I believed he had gone to the utmost limits of his authority. He replied that he had done all that he could, and drew attention to the fact that he had buried all of the *Maine's* men in the same plot of ground, without respect to creed, Protestant or Catholic. It was quite true, and the ground was given for all time to the United States, without expense. After the funeral, I sent the following telegram to the Navy Department:

Nineteen of *Maine's* dead were buried this afternoon, with great civil, ecclesiastical, naval, and military ceremonies, and with all the resources of Havana brought into requisition. The Spanish government, under express directions of General Blanco, the Bishop of Havana, General Parrado, Admiral Manterola, and the mayor of Havana, took complete charge of all arrangements. The bodies were first laid in state in the building of the civil government of Havana, where they were covered with floral and other emblems suitable to the occasion, which were presented by officials and other persons of Havana, of all shades of political opinion. They were escorted to the cemetery by representatives of all military, naval, and civil organizations, and foreign consular officers, and through a vast concourse of people spreading over the route. General Lee, myself, and officers and men of the *Maine* now here, together with Lieutenant-Commander

The Explosion

Cowles and members of the *Fern's* crew, were given special carriages and conveniences. Ground for the burial of all the *Maine's* dead has been presented by General Blanco and the Bishop of Havana. The utmost sympathy and respect have been shown. I am informed by the authorities that this is the second instance only of such a demonstration having been shown to foreigners in the history of Havana. It is inconceivable that a greater demonstration could have been made. To me personally a great number of people have expressed sympathy for the *Maine* and for the United States government and people. The remainder of the dead must, perforce, be buried with brief ceremony, which will be conducted by ourselves, but the care and preparation of the remains will be with the Spanish authorities. About forty in addition to those buried have come ashore to-day. Very few are now recognizable. Even in the case of some of those who are hurt, but live, recognition is difficult. I have not for a moment lost sight of the grief of the families and friends of the members of my crew, but I beg the department to explain to them that it is impracticable, in fact impossible, to send bodies home. Facilities are lacking, and embalmment is necessary to secure shipment, even under the most favorable circumstances. Embalming is only imperfectly done here. Will wire all cases of identification. I maintain organization among my small force here, but it can be well understood that the execution of the work with which we are charged is one of much detail and difficult of execution. It is believed that all of the department's telegrams have reached me. I am deeply grateful for the helpful sentiments and directions telegraphed by the President and the department. I have the earnest help of all the officers of the *Maine* now here, which was to be expected under all circumstances. A previous telegram sent to-day gives the names of those buried by the Spanish authorities. The flags of all vessels, naval and merchant, in Havana harbor have been at half-mast yesterday and to-day. Shall send *Mangrove* back to Key West to-morrow with eight wounded. Will wire names later. Dr. Clendenin of the army will remain with the wounded. Assistant Surgeon Spear also came with the *Mangrove*, but will be detained here on board the *Fern*, to accompany others of the wounded when they are ready to be removed. Will put some divers at work to-morrow. Divers requested of Admiral Sicard will be here Saturday morning by the *Olivette*. Recovery of *Maine's* battery impracticable, except by regular wrecking outfit.

The burial of those nineteen men ended the official demonstration on the part of the Spaniards, which was proper. Thereafter, having been furnished the facilities for subsequent burials, we were allowed to proceed in our own way. Chaplain Chidwick, assisted by a most devoted and kind-hearted undertaker, a Spaniard, identified the bodies, and saw them prepared for the grave. After that he conducted the burials so long as we continued to inter the bodies at Havana. When it became possible to forward them to Key West by steamer, they were sent in that way and buried at Key West. Surgeon Heneberger gave his attention to the wounded and to mortuary statistics, while Paymaster Ray quietly, and with the greatest promptness, managed the financial intricacies of the situation.

I felt that I took upon myself a great moral responsibility in burying the *Maine's* dead at

GRAVE OF THE "MAINE'S" DEAD IN THE CEMETERY AT HAVANA.

The Explosion

Havana; but in the tropics it was necessary to bury the dead very promptly, which may well be imagined. Fault was found with me on some sides by a few patriotic citizens of the United States for permitting the Spanish authorities to bury our dead; but I thought that I knew the administration of our government and the people of the United States well enough to count on their approval of my course as the only one practicable in the circumstances in which we were so unfortunately placed. Results showed that I was not mistaken.

It is exceedingly difficult for the American mind to comprehend certain subsequent proceedings of the Spanish officials. It can be explained only on the ground that Spanish authority in Cuba has so long been dominant and exacting that Spanish officials do not know how to unbend in a practical way, as we understand it, however much they may concede in the way of sentiment and sympathy. I have stated that on the night of the disaster I requested the captain of the cruiser *Alfonso XII* to place patrol-boats about the *Maine* to guard her from intrusion. The request was complied with, and thereafter, for many days, the Spanish boats kept up their patrol. Nobody was allowed to approach the wreck without proper authority; but at first their vigilance extended, adversely, even to the captain and officers of the *Maine*.

On the first or second day after the explosion, I myself attempted to go on board the wreck. I was stopped by a Spanish patrol-boat, which refused to allow me on board, even when it was explained that I was the captain of the *Maine*. My first impulse was to ignore the boats and force a passage on board; but, on second thought, I went on board the *Alfonso XII*, and suggested to her captain that the Spanish boats had misconceived their orders, since they had declined to allow me to board the wreck. The captain explained that it was simply a matter of identification, and that he would give me certain passes for myself and officers whereby I could pass the patrol. I approved this plan on the ground that, having asked him to set the patrol, it was only proper that I should support him in demanding complete identification. But I could not understand why passes had not been sent me before.

Shortly afterward I became very much concerned at the slow recovery of bodies. It was evident that many were down in the wreck. I knew that relatives and friends would be urgent at the Navy Department, and it was very necessary to respect their sentiments. I felt it very keenly. At the American consulate I had met certain Cuban divers, and arranged that they should visit me the next day with a view to going down in the *Maine* for the recovery of bodies. These divers afterward disposed of their services to an American newspaper correspondent, who visited me in their company. He offered — as I then knew, by direction of his paper — to send down the divers entirely at the expense of his paper, for the avowed purpose of recovering the dead. I suspected at the time that his paper had directed him to make an investigation of the wreck of the *Maine*. Of course I declined any effort to anticipate the official investigation; but finally, when the correspondent surrendered his divers to me and placed them absolutely under my direction, I sent them over to the wreck with an officer, with instructions to allow them to make a descent, under his superintendence, for the sole purpose of recovering bodies. The party was stopped by the Spanish boats with the remark that "no American diver could go down without a Spanish diver, and no Spanish diver without an American diver."

I also was not allowed to go on board to hoist the national ensign. This was taking charge of matters unjustifiably. In respect to these several hindrances, I had received no notification in advance. However grateful I was for the good offices of the Spanish officials, I could not concede such a state of things. Shortly after these incidents, and while I was preparing to visit the *Alfonso XII* to protest, her captain chanced to come aboard the *Fern* to make a return visit of ceremony, I believe, to that vessel's commander, Lieutenant-Commander Cowles. I stated the case to the Spanish captain, and asked if the Spanish boatmen had misconstrued his orders. He was requested to take such measures as would insure me thereafter access to the wreck of the *Maine* without any interference, on the presentation of a pass or identification paper. He was somewhat embarrassed, and courteously explained that he was obeying the orders of Admiral Manterola, to whom I should appeal. I assured him that I fully realized that he must obey his orders, and said that I would carry the case higher. Then the conversation was changed to more agreeable topics.

It was not my intention to apply to the Admiral, because I felt that the case should be taken from the hands of subordinates. The matter was reported to General Lee, who made an appointment for us with Captain and Governor-General Blanco. When we visited General Blanco, there were present, besides himself,

German. Newton. Eiermann. Metz. Marston. Bonner.

THE "MAINE'S" BASEBALL NINE AS ORGANIZED AT THE TIME OF THE EXPLOSION.

All were lost with the exception of Bloomer. Newton was the ship's bugler and sounded taps just before the explosion. The goat was left behind at Key West.

The Explosion

only Dr. Congosto, General Lee, and myself. General Lee recited the circumstances to which I have already referred; he did it gravely and with due composure. Although outwardly composed, I was naturally indignant that an officer in my difficult position should be hedged in with vexatious restrictions, and determined to demand that they be ended. I suggested to General Lee that I, as a naval officer, understood international comity as applying to my command, for which reason I hoped that he would trust me to state my view of the case. He at once complied.

I then reminded General Blanco, through Dr. Congosto, who acted as interpreter, that the *Maine* had entered the port of Havana with, at least, the implied assent of the Spanish government; that having so entered, she was constructively under the protection of the Spanish government and entitled to extraterritorial courtesy and to exemptions from local jurisdiction and control, as recognized in international law. So far as her internal affairs were concerned, she was entitled, under international usage and courtesy, to be considered a part of the territory of her own country, and under the direction of her own commanding officer, who was responsible to his government. Nevertheless, an attempt

The "Maine"

had been made to keep me out of my command while my pennant was flying at the masthead; and Admiral Manterola had undertaken to say when I could or could not be permitted to visit my command. I stated further that so long as my pennant flew I could yield no part of my responsibility without orders, and I hoped he would remove restrictions.

General Blanco urged that there should be a joint investigation; that a Spanish law required a Spanish investigation, and Spanish honor was involved. To which I replied that I recognized that the Spanish government had a moral right to investigate the loss of the *Maine*, but that any investigation by the Spanish government within the ship should, properly, be pursued after an appeal directly to the United States government. I said that although I did not believe the United States would consent to a joint investigation, it was probable that the government would desire that Spain should have an opportunity to make an independent investigation.

General Lee took the same ground, and entered into the discussion generally. We both agreed that we should take pleasure in approving to the United States government an independent investigation by the Spanish government. General Blanco yielded with the remark

The Explosion

that, if the interior of the vessel was subject to the control of the United States, the outside was under the control of Spain. I then said that I should refrain from exploring the harbor. Dr. Congosto replied with some spirit, "You may, if you like." Knowing that the remark should not be taken seriously, I again disclaimed any intention of pursuing our operations into the region surrounding the *Maine*.

The interview was ended pleasantly with the promise of General Blanco to issue immediate orders to Admiral Manterola to give me access to the *Maine* thereafter. That day the United States national ensign was hoisted, and then hauled down to half-mast, where it remained always, day and night, during the remainder of my stay at Havana. The ensign on board a national ship is hauled down at sundown, and is not again hoisted until eight o'clock the following morning. Since the *Maine* was blown up at 9:40 P. M., it is apparent why her flag was not up until I hoisted it on that occasion. In keeping it up, day and night, I desired to make it clear that interference with the ship was interference with the flag. Most of the photographs of the wreck of the *Maine* show the flag at half-mast.

The incident which I have related made my position stronger thereafter, so far as pertained to my own control of the *Maine*. It was not again questioned until just before my departure from Havana.

Notwithstanding the sympathy with the survivors of the *Maine* evinced in Havana, the local press was not friendly. Certain papers made petty and unfavorable remarks about me, quite different from those in the press of the United States in respect to Captain Eulate personally, when the *Vizcaya* visited New York, while the excitement over the loss of the *Maine* was at its highest. On the other hand, a part of our press was merciless toward the Spaniards generally, and this did not tend to make more comfortable the position of the survivors of the *Maine* at Havana. There was reason to believe that the tone of these papers was galling to the Spaniards.

At the funeral of nineteen men of the *Maine* on February 19, I had worn a civilian's sack suit. I had nothing else. Lieutenant-Commander Cowles of the *Fern* was in uniform, and quite generally passed as Captain Sigsbee. One of the Havana papers — one can hardly say newspapers — made a sneering comment, even at that time, at my having appeared in uniform, although my uniform had been reported lost. The Spanish press has persisted in declaring that I and many

MINSTREL GROUP WHO PERFORMED AT THE ENTERTAINMENT GIVEN BY THE CREW OF THE "MAINE" TO THE CREW OF THE "COLUMBIA."

The sailor with tall hat and striped shirt is Walsh, coxswain of the captain's gig, who was killed; the man in cook's costume at the right, private marine Joseph Luts, was saved, and is now Captain Sigsbee's orderly on board the *Texas*.

The Explosion

other officers of the *Maine* were not on board at the time of the explosion. Spanish officials everywhere in Havana knew to the contrary. I have been informed that a Spanish officer, on the eve of leaving the United States, where he had been a prisoner, having been captured in honorable fight, thought fit to assert that I had wept in Havana, and deplored the ending of my naval career. The report seems incredible, and it would be undignified to deny so absurd a statement. My own reserve heretofore has not failed of appreciation on the Spanish side. After the war was opened, a Spanish officer of high rank at Havana sent me his kind regards by returned prisoners.

On February 20 I visited the San Ambrosio Hospital to see the wounded men. There had been some cases of yellow fever at the hospital, and we felt concern at that fact, but there was probably no hospital in Havana where yellow fever had not been present at one time or another.

There can be no doubt that the Spaniards gave us the benefit of the best they had at their disposal. To enter the ward where our men were installed it was necessary to pass through a ward of Spanish invalids, many of whom appeared to be convalescent. At the entrance of the ward set aside for our use there was exhibited a characteristic bit of Spanish courtesy. On the wall was a placard demanding that all who entered that room should remove their hats. I visited each cot and talked with each patient, asked his location on board the *Maine* at the time of the explosion, his sensations and experiences, and wished him speedy recovery. They seemed delighted to welcome me, and said pleasant things, in forgetfulness of their own sufferings. At that hospital, Andrew V. Erikson, seaman, and Carl A. Smith, seaman, had died on the 18th, Alfred J. Holland, cockswain, on the 19th, and Harry Jectson, seaman, and Frank Fisher, ordinary seaman, on the day of my visit. George A. Koebler, apprentice, first-class, and Frederick C. Holzer, ordinary seaman, both young and excellent men, were very low.

Koebler was a handsome, cheery, willing, and capable apprentice, equally a pronounced favorite forward and aft. When there was doubt as to the proper man to employ for any confidential service, young Koebler was generally selected. He was in everything that was going on, on board the *Maine*, and had lately been married in Brooklyn, New York. It was his habit to come to me occasionally and ask my advice in his private affairs. I found that he accepted

The Explosion

it and acted upon it. He was delirious during my visit, but in some way became aware of my presence as soon as I entered the ward. He kept calling for me, so I visited him out of his regular turn. Imagining that the *Maine* was to go to New Orleans and leave him at the hospital, he declared that he was able to go on board, that it was not right to leave him there, and appealed to me to take him with me. But he became perfectly quiet and resigned when I assured him that the *Maine* should never leave Havana without him. It was very affecting. Poor fellow! he died on the 22d.

Holzer seemed in better condition than Koebler, and gave us the hope that he would recover. His mind was clear. When I took his hand he said: "Captain, I'm sorry such bad luck has come upon you." I replied: "Thank you, Holzer; I fear you have sailed with the wrong captain this time." He disputed the point with such nice consideration that my hope for him was strengthened, but he died on the 25th. Holzer was Chaplain Chidwick's assistant at religious services; the chaplain had a high regard for him, and felt his loss keenly, as we all did.

It was not until February 23 that I managed to read newspapers from the United States. The tone of the press toward me and the officers and

The "Maine"

men surprised and pleased me. It was sympathetic and commendatory, and without rebuke. The importance attached to my first telegram was far beyond my anticipation. Although I had hoped that some good effect might flow from the despatch, it had not entered my mind that it would reflect on me in a laudatory sense. It was hardly possible that a captain who had just lost his ship should look further than exoneration so soon afterward.

Ensign Powelson (witness).
Captain Sampson.   Lt.-Com. Potter.

Captain Chadwick.   The Judge-Advocate, Lt.-Com. Marix.   Official Stenographer.

THE COURT OF INQUIRY ON BOARD THE "MANGROVE"

III

THE WRECKING AND THE INQUIRY

MUCH interest was excited by the arrival in Havana of the first lot of American newspapers received after the loss of the *Maine*. A Spanish officer of high rank whom I visited showed me a New York paper of February 17 in which was pictured the *Maine* anchored over a mine. On another page was a plan showing wires leading from the *Maine* to the shore. The officer asked me what I thought of that. It was explained that we had no censorship in the United States; that each person applied his own criticism to what he saw and read in the papers. Apparently the Spanish officer could not grasp the idea. The interview was not at all unfriendly, and he took it in good part when it was pointed out that the Havana newspapers were very unfair toward me, without respect to my situation in their port. I asserted that if the

The "Maine"

American newspapers gave more than the news, the Spanish newspapers gave less than the news: it was a question of choice.

When the Spanish officer reverted to those illustrations of the *Maine*, I argued in this wise: The *Maine* blew up at 9:40 P. M. on the 15th; the news reached the United States very early on the morning of the 16th. This newspaper went to press about 3 A. M. on the morning of the 17th. It took time to draw those pictures and reproduce them. The inference was clear: the newspaper must have been possessed of a knowledge of the mine before the *Maine* was blown up. Therefore it disturbed me to guess why I had not been told of the danger. This had the required effect, and the newspaper was dropped out of the conversation.

The American newspaper correspondent in Havana was a bugaboo to the Spaniards, from the censor to others all along the line. Nobody but the censor seemed to be able to stop him, and even the censor could not control more than the cable despatches. I remember that one correspondent complained that he was not allowed to say that Captain Sigsbee was *reticent*. He was made to say that Captain Sigsbee was reserved. The censor thought it a question of courtesy. The correspondents were active, ener-

The Wrecking and the Inquiry

getic, and even aggressive in their efforts to get all the news. The people of the United States demanded the news, and they got it. It was soon plain to me that the correspondents were under strict orders from their papers — orders more mandatory and difficult of execution than those commonly issued in the naval service. Very early I applied a certain rule of conduct to these gentlemen, and it worked to perfection. I never impugned their motives, nor denied myself to them when it was possible to see them, never misled them, nor gave any one correspondent the "start in the running." If I had news that could properly be given, I gave it. If what I knew could not be given, I so informed them frankly. I could not give "interviews." My acquaintanceship extended to every American correspondent in Havana. No more sincere sympathy, consideration, and forbearance were shown me than by these correspondents. During the sittings of the court of inquiry, when I could not properly converse on the subject of the investigations, I gave them no word of

SURVIVORS AT THE HOSPITAL, KEY WEST, MAKING THE INITIAL OF THE LOST SHIP.

news, which they were under extreme pressure to provide. Their approval in the matter was expressed both sentimentally and tangibly when I was leaving Havana, of which more later.

Every mail brought me many letters from the United States and abroad. In the aggregate there were hundreds of them. More than half were letters of approval and commendation. Many were from the families of the dead and wounded men. The latter were answered at once; the former so far as opportunity permitted, but many remain unanswered because of the constant emergency, both great and small, that has pressed upon me since the loss of the *Maine*. I read every letter from mourning relatives, but the harrowing nature of their contents made it absolutely impossible for me to answer them personally, burdened as I was by urgent and unwonted duties. It was touching to note that most of them contained apologies for appealing to me while I was pressed with other duties. They were indorsed with suitable directions as to writing or telegraphing, and then given over to Chaplain Chidwick and Naval Cadet Holden for reply. From what I have written, it may be inferred that Chaplain Chidwick did this duty thoroughly well. So did Mr. Hol-

ENSIGN W. V. N. POWELSON, U. S. N.

The Wrecking and the Inquiry

den; he was my right hand, in many ways, at Havana, and saved me much work and anxiety. His judgment, ability, and sense of duty and loyalty were strikingly admirable. He is one of the best examples of what the Naval Academy can produce when the basic material is of the right kind.

My personal relations with General Blanco and Admiral Manterola, and, in fact, with all the Spanish officials, remained cordial until the last; there was no interruption whatever. Soon after the explosion I received a personal visit from Admiral Manterola at the Hotel Inglaterra. He was accompanied by his aide, a lieutenant in the Spanish navy. Our interpreter was a very intelligent clerk of the hotel, Mr. Gonzales. Admiral Manterola had ordered an inquiry, on the part of the Spanish government, into the cause of the explosion. We talked freely, because I desired to let it be known that I had no fear of an investigation, and believed that the United States would be impartial.

The admiral assumed from the first that the explosion was from the interior of the vessel. He asked if the dynamo-boilers had not exploded. I told him we had no dynamo-boilers. He said that the plans of the vessel, as published, showed that the guncotton store-room, or magazine, was

The "Maine"

forward near the zone of the explosion. He was informed that those plans had been changed, and that the guncotton was stowed aft, under the captain's cabin, where the vessel was virtually intact. He pointed out that modern gunpowders were sometimes very unstable. This was met by the remark that our powder was of the old and stable brown prismatic kind, and that we had no fancy powder. He referred to the probable effect of boilers, lighted, near the forward coal-bunkers, which were adjacent to the magazines. This again was met with the remark that for three months no boiler in the forward boiler-compartment had been lighted; that while in port the two aftermost boilers in the ship had been doing service.

Apparently Admiral Manterola was not inclined to accept anything but an interior cause. I remarked that our own investigation would be exhaustive, and that every possible interior cause would be included. He seemed desirous of knowing the tendency of my views, and I was equally concerned to know what he thought. I ventured to say that a few persons of evil disposition, with conveniences at hand, if so inclined, could have blown up the *Maine* from the outside; that there were bad men everywhere as well as good men. He turned to the interpreter and

The Wrecking and the Inquiry

said something which I could not understand; evidently he did not like that view. I caught enough of the interpreter's protest to him, and also of the aide's, to understand that they advised him to be conciliatory toward me. Their glances were directed toward him to the same effect. I appeared not to observe anything unusual, but went on to say that any investigation which did

KEY RECOVERED FROM THE WRECK OF THE "MAINE"

not consider all possible exterior causes, as well as all possible interior causes, would not be accepted as exhaustive, and that the United States government would not come to any conclusion in advance as to whether the cause was exterior or interior. Admiral Manterola conceded the point very politely, and soon after the visit terminated in the usual friendly way.

On the afternoon of March 1 there was a great

The "Maine"

demonstration on the water and along the waterfront. Aërial bombs were thrown up for some hours, and the excitement intensified toward sundown. Shortly after sunset the Spanish armored cruiser *Vizcaya* arrived from New York. Her entrance excited great enthusiasm among the Spaniards. Many boats and steamers were present to give her welcome. There were streamers and flags flying on shore, and the wharves were crowded with people. It was reported to me that there were cries of "Down with the Americans!" It was different from an American demonstration; it was childlike, even pathetic. Lieutenant-Commander Cowles of the *Fern* and I went on shore in the thick of the crowd, and, pressing through the narrow gateway leading from the Machina to the city streets, pursued our way quite as usual. After the arrival of the *Vizcaya* Americans at Havana remained serene in the knowledge of that fine fleet over at Tortugas. The *Maine* was a thing of the past, but the fleet was a thing of the future. By that time the atmosphere at Havana was waxing volcanic with the promise of war, but the Spaniards apparently gave no heed to our fleet, which could then have destroyed Havana in short order.

Lieutenant-Commander Cowles, as the junior

HAVANA PASSENGER BOATS AROUND THE SPANISH CRUISER "VIZCAYA" ON A VISITING DAY

The Wrecking and the Inquiry

in rank, made the first visit of ceremony to Captain Eulate of the *Vizcaya*, and informed him that I was quartered on board the *Fern*. Captain Eulate then visited me on board. I was in citizen's clothes, having lost all my uniforms. A seaman of the *Fern* interpreted for us. Captain Eulate addressed himself chiefly to Lieutenant-Commander Cowles until the interpreter chanced to mention my name, when Captain Eulate turned in surprise and asked if I was Captain Sigsbee of the *Maine*. He took in the situation at once, arose, and, with an exclamation, threw his arms about me and gave expression to his sympathy. He afterward spoke pleasantly of his rather extensive acquaintance with United States naval officers.

On March 5 the Spanish armored cruiser *Almirante Oquendo*, a sister ship of the *Vizcaya*, arrived at Havana amid demonstrations similar to those which had greeted the *Vizcaya*. Then the Spanish element of the populace was steeped in happiness and contentment. The lost power of the sunken *Maine* was manifestly exceeded by that of the Spanish ships. Assuredly there was much reason for their exhibition of pride, for the Spanish cruisers were fine specimens of naval architecture. They were visited day after day by the people of Havana, and were, therefore,

The "Maine"

almost constantly surrounded by boats during visiting-hours. The two cruisers were much alike. A bead or molding under the coat of arms on the stern was painted black on one and yellow on the other, and this was about as striking a distinction as could be observed. Once when I remarked to Captain Eulate the similarity, he smiled and claimed there was a difference in his favor: the *Vizcaya* had a silk flag and some Galician bagpipers, which the *Oquendo* had not.

After the arrival of the *Vizcaya* I was informed that the *Fern* would soon leave Havana to take food to the reconcentrados in other ports. It was intended that I and others, including the divers, should quarter ourselves aboard the *Mangrove*. I reported to Rear-Admiral Sicard that the *Mangrove* had not quarters sufficient for us. It was necessary to safeguard the health of the divers very carefully; their work in the foul water of the harbor compelled this. It was also pointed out that I would be left without uniformed officers to employ for naval visits and courtesies. Accordingly, the *Montgomery*, Commander George A. Converse, arrived on March 9, to relieve the *Fern*, which left the same day. The *Montgomery*, a handsome and efficient ship, presented a fine appearance from the city.

This relief of vessels gave rise to an incident

The Wrecking and the Inquiry

which, by confusion, has produced the impression, rather wide-spread in the United States, that the *Maine's* berth was shifted by the Spanish officials after her arrival at Havana. It has already been stated that she remained continuously at the same mooring-buoy. The *Fern* had been lying at the buoy nearest the Machina and the wreck of the *Maine*, No. 4 of Chart 307, the same that had served for the *Alfonso XII* prior to the explosion. In expectation of the arrival of the *Montgomery*, the *Fern* had procured a pilot in the forenoon of the 9th. The prospective coming of the *Montgomery* had been announced to the Spanish officials, and it had been arranged with the pilot that the *Montgomery* should succeed to the *Fern's* buoy. To avoid confusion, the *Fern* vacated the buoy several hours in advance and rode to her own anchor near the wreck. As soon as she had shifted her berth, a Spanish naval officer, representing the captain of the port, visited the *Fern*, and informed me that a buoy to the southward of the wreck, No. 6 of Chart 307, would be given to the *Montgomery*, as the *Alfonso XII* was under orders from Admiral Manterola to take the moorings vacated by the *Fern*. I at once sent an officer to Admiral Manterola with a note requesting that the *Montgomery* be permitted to take the *Fern's* buoy,—

in view of its close proximity to the wreck, — if consistent with the necessities of the Spanish ship. The *Alfonso XII* reached the buoy before the officer reached the admiral. A prompt reply was returned, saying that the change had been made in order that the Spanish cruiser might be near the Machina, which was more convenient for the prosecution of work on her boilers, but that she would be moved back if I so desired. Before I could make known my wishes the *Alfonso XII* hauled off and took another berth. I then visited Admiral Manterola personally, and requested that the *Alfonso XII* keep the *Fern's* buoy, and that I be permitted to anchor the *Montgomery* where the *Fern* was then lying. The admiral declined to entertain the proposition, courteously insisting that the *Montgomery* should have the desired buoy. He stated that the captain of the port had mistaken his orders, or that there had been a misunderstanding of some kind. The *Montgomery* took the buoy when she arrived later in the day. Frankly, I preferred that buoy for the further reason that it had been used for the *Alfonso XII*, from which I judged that the berth would be free from harbor-defense mines, if any existed.

I had received no assurance that the harbor was not mined, and was of the opinion that the

THE "MONTGOMERY" SALUTING AFTER MOORING AT HAVANA.

The Wrecking and the Inquiry

Maine had been blown up from the outside, irrespective of any attachment of culpability to the Spanish authorities. It had been made sufficiently plain that those authorities were not taking measures to safeguard our vessels. There were two ways of regarding this omission: first, that they believed that there was no need for safeguarding; secondly, that if there was need, they would not, as a question of policy, seem to make the admission. The proceedings of the Spanish commission to investigate the loss of the *Maine* show that Spanish boats kept a patrol about the floating dry-dock. It would have been mincing matters to infer that I had not the right to act in all proper ways according to any suspicions, just or unjust. The situation in which I found myself was not one to inspire me with perfect trust in my fellow-men. There being no proof of culpability in any direction, suspicion was the logical guide to precautionary measures.

I regretted the assignment of so valuable a ship as the *Montgomery* to service in Havana, notwithstanding she was sent to support me in my wishes for naval environment. The *Fern* was preferred as sufficiently serving the purpose. However, I took up my quarters on board the *Montgomery*, where I received the kind attentions of Commander Converse.

The "Maine"

The first night of the *Montgomery* in port was marked by a ludicrous incident — ludicrous in the termination, although rather serious in its first stage of development. About 8 P. M. Commander Converse and I had decided to go in company to make a visit of courtesy to the members of the court of inquiry on board the *Mangrove*. The gig had been called away when Commander Converse informed me that a most remarkable tapping sound had been reported from the lower forward compartments of the ship, but could not be precisely located. We were heading to the eastward, broadside to broadside with the *Vizcaya*, which was on our port beam and very near. We resolved to investigate. Continued reports were demanded. The sound grew in distinctness; there was a regular tapping like that of an electrical transmitter. I recommended that the beats be timed. They were two hundred and forty a minute — a multiple of sixty; therefore, clockwork. That was serious. The crew, being forward, did not like the appearance of things: they did not mind square fighting, but clockwork under the keel was not to their liking. There were some of the survivors of the *Maine* on board, including the captain. I called for more reports, and directed that some one's ear be applied to the riding-cable, and that

The Wrecking and the Inquiry

a boat be sent to listen at the mooring-buoy, to note if the sound was transmitted through the water. The sound grew in volume, and could be located under a port compartment, well forward. A boat was sent outside to probe with an oar. Nothing was discovered. The bounds of patience were no longer conterminous with the limits of international courtesy, so the bottom of the ship was swept with a rope by means of boats. Other boats were sent to ride at the extreme ends of the lower booms by way of patrol.

I lost my temper, and remarked that one might get as well used to blowing up as to hanging, but once was enough. The tapping never ceased, but began to draw slowly aft. It was reported as most distinct at the port gangway, then was heard most clearly in the port shaft-alley, which was abaft the gangway. Here was the suggestion of a solution. The *Montgomery's* heading was noted: she was slowly swinging, head to the southward; so was the *Vizcaya*. A man was sent to note if the sound continued in the forward compartment. It had ceased. The cause was clear: the sound had continued to be most audible in that part of the *Montgomery* that was nearest the *Vizcaya*, as the vessels swung at their moorings. It came from the *Vizcaya* through the water. Commander

Converse and I had heroically resolved to remain on board and take our chances. We remained on board, but not heroically. A day or two afterward, when Captain Eulate came on board, we told him of our "scare," to our mutual amusement. He said that the number of beats a minute showed that the sound came from his dynamo or from his circulating-pump.

I have already mentioned that the Spanish men-of-war were vigilant in certain directions as to themselves and not to the *Montgomery*. My orders to make a friendly visit had not been countermanded. I lived up to them, to the best of my ability, but the situation was daily growing more tense. Immutable law seemed to be impelling Spain and the United States toward war. While abhorring war, as causing more severe and sustained suffering among women and children than among combatant men, I grew gradually into such a condition of mind that I, in common with many of my fellow-countrymen, was not averse to war with Spain.

During the latter part of the visit of the *Montgomery* I believed that her presence in Havana was no longer desirable. Unless she was protected from without, she was unnecessarily risked. The presence in the harbor of the *Vizcaya* and

WRECKING WITH THE AID OF HYDRAULIC JACKS

The Wrecking and the Inquiry

the *Oquendo* offset any moral effect that could be produced by a single United States war-vessel. It was then my opinion that no United States naval force should be employed at Havana unless aggressively, and outside the harbor. It had become impossible for the United States to fly its flag in security for the protection of its citizens. In that connection one could well "remember the *Maine.*" I recommended that the *Montgomery* be ordered away; she was relieved by the *Fern* on March 17, and Lieutenant-Commander Wainwright and I transferred ourselves to the *Fern.*

It was not my habit at Havana to court serious conversation as to Spanish policies, but, naturally, the views of people of different shades of opinion came to me. Intelligent Cubans declared that Spain desired war with the United States as the most honorable way of relinquishing Cuba. They said that Spain had been preparing for the former event for two years, and pointed to the strong fortifications on the seafront and the absence of fortifications on the land side of the city. A Cuban lawyer of the highest standing, who was closely connected with the politics of the island, and who was willing to accept some degree of Spanish sovereignty, asserted to me that Spain would fight without regard to consequences; that she would fight even though she knew that she would be defeated. He appeared to base his belief chiefly on the character of the Spanish people. I was always very cautious as to expressing any opinions of my own. I received views without giving them. In reply to annexation sentiments, it was my custom to say that annexation was not a public question in the United States.

Soon after the destruction of the *Maine*, a gentleman came to me in the Hotel Inglaterra and tendered me a letter of sympathy from General Maximo Gomez, commander-in-chief of the Cuban army. When the letter was read I expressed my gratitude for the sentiments of General Gomez and accepted them, but asked that the delivery of the letter be deferred until my departure from Havana. It was delivered as requested.

The *Maine* sank in from five and a half to six fathoms of water, and day by day settled in the mud until the poop-deck was about four feet under water. The first matter to engross the attention of the government and of the officers of the vessel was the care of the wounded, the recovery and burial of the dead, and the circulation of information among the relatives of the officers and crew. Next followed the ques-

The Wrecking and the Inquiry

tion of wrecking the vessel. Her value when she arrived at Havana, with everything on board, was about five million dollars. Even a casual inspection of the wreck made it clear that little could be done beyond investigation and the recovery of the dead, except by the employment of the means of a wrecking company. The *Mangrove* removed certain parts of the armament and equipment, and navy divers were sent from the fleet at Key West to do the preliminary work of searching the wreck. Every naval vessel of large size is provided with a diving outfit and has one or more men trained to dive in armor. The government promptly began negotiations with wrecking organizations, and, as soon as these negotiations took form, Lieutenant-Commander Wainwright was put in charge of the wrecking operations and represented the government in dealing with the wrecking companies. Thereafter he was daily on or about the wreck, at great risk to his health.

At first, bodies were found almost from hour to hour, and were buried as soon as prepared for burial. It was a sad sight at the Machina landing, where bodies were to be seen in the water alongside the sea-wall at all times. To relieve the public eye of this condition of affairs, a large lighter was obtained and anchored near the wreck. On its deck there was always a great pile of burial-cases. To this lighter all bodies were then taken as soon as recovered, and after being prepared for burial, were at first taken to the Colon Cemetery, and toward the last to Key West; in the latter case they were generally carried by the Coast Survey steamer *Bache*, commanded by Lieutenant-Commander William J. Barnette, U. S. N.

The work of the naval divers, chiefly a work of investigation, occupied about five weeks, and was commonly directed at the zone of explosion, down in the forward part of the wreck. The water of Havana harbor, although filthy, is not so bad in winter as in summer. Our men went down willingly and did excellent service. After each diver had completed his labors for the day he was thoroughly washed with disinfectants. Everything taken from the wreck, except articles of unwieldy size, was plunged into a disinfecting solution. It was recommended by Surgeon Heneberger of the *Maine*, after conference with Surgeon Brunner of the United States Marine Hospital Service and others, that no article of textile fabric should be used on recovery, but that all should either be burned or given to the acclimated poor of Havana. This recommendation was adopted, and the survivors of the

The Wrecking and the Inquiry

Maine lost all of their clothing. Assistant Surgeon Spear was in charge of the disinfecting processes.

February 19 was an eventful day. The *Bache* had arrived with divers the day before, but this day the *Olivette* brought more divers and further outfits. Ensign Frank H. Brumby and Gunner Charles Morgan arrived from the fleet to assist at the wreck. I sent the following telegram to the Navy Department:

> . . . One hundred and twenty-five coffins, containing one hundred and twenty-five dead, now buried; nine ready for burial to-morrow. . . .

And the following telegram was received by General Lee from the Department of State at Washington:

> The government of the United States has already begun an investigation as to the causes of the disaster to the *Maine*, through officers of the navy specially appointed for that purpose, which will proceed independently.
>
> The government will afford every facility it can to the Spanish authorities in whatever investigation they may see fit to make upon their part.

This despatch disposed of the question of joint investigation. This day funeral services were held at the cathedral over the remains of the Spanish colonel Ruiz, who had been killed in

The "Maine"

December by order of an insurgent colonel. I desired to attend the funeral with General Lee, in recognition of the public demonstration of sympathy for our dead made by the Spaniards, but reluctantly abandoned my intention because I had no suitable garments to wear. Convention is strictly drawn by the Spaniards in regard to funerals, and one must wear uniform or civilian's evening dress; I had neither.

On the 21st the *Mangrove* returned from Key West, bringing the members of the court of inquiry, and the court convened on board that vessel. I was the first witness. The court was composed of Captain William T. Sampson, at that time in command of the battle-ship *Iowa;* Captain French E. Chadwick, captain of the flagship *New York;* and Lieutenant-Commander William P. Potter, executive officer of the *New York.* The judge-advocate was Lieutenant-Commander Adolph Marix, who has already been mentioned as having been at one time executive officer of the *Maine.* It was a court which inspired confidence. All the members were scholarly men. Admiral Sampson had been at the head of the torpedo station, superintendent of the Naval Academy, and chief of the Bureau of Ordnance. Captain Chadwick had been United States naval attaché at London,

EXPERT DIVER ANDREW OLSEN PREPARING TO DESCEND.

The Wrecking and the Inquiry

and chief of the Bureau of Equipment. Lieutenant-Commander Potter had held various positions of importance, especially at the Naval Academy. Lieutenant-Commander Marix knew the structure of the *Maine* and her organization in every detail; in fact, under a former commanding officer, Captain Arent S. Crowninshield (now chief of the Bureau of Navigation of the Navy Department), he organized the crew of the vessel. He is a highly intelligent, active, and decisive officer. As commanding officer of the *Maine* at the time of her destruction, I was, in a measure, under fire by the court. The constitution of the court pleased me greatly. I desired to have the facts investigated, not only on their merits, but in a way to be convincing to the public, and I was sure that this court of inquiry would deal with the case exhaustively.

On the same day Commander Peral of the Spanish court of inquiry visited the *Mangrove* while I was on board, and conversed on various matters. I had already provided him with plans of the *Maine*, in order that he might be prepared to pursue his independent investigation without loss of time. General Lee informed General Blanco of the expected arrival of wrecking-vessels, and no obstacle was put in the way of prosecuting the wrecking work.

The "Maine"

During the day various articles were recovered from my cabins: the silverware presented to the vessel by the State of Maine, my bicycle, a typewriting machine, etc. The after-superstructure, in which were my cabins, was the only part of the vessel which was easily accessible to the divers. Below that all was confusion. Everything that was buoyant, including mattresses and furniture, had risen to the ceiling, blocking the hatches. There was some comment as to the recovery of my bicycle. I presume it was in the way of the diver, and he got rid of it by passing it out; or he may have intended to do me a kindness. It was ruined for riding, of course. But I find I have omitted to mention that certain articles of greater importance were recovered. The first work done by the divers was to secure these articles.

My earliest effort by means of the divers was to secure the navy cipher code and the signal-books. In this we were successful. Next the magazine and shell-room keys were sought. They had hung at the foot of my bunk, on hooks, near the ceiling. At the first attempt the diver failed to get them. His failure gave me more of a shock than the explosion itself. A missing key might have meant that a magazine had been entered against my knowledge, or that some

The Wrecking and the Inquiry

diver had been down at night and secured the key. It was a case of treachery on board or of an invitation to war. Lieutenant-Commander Wainwright questioned the diver very closely, and concluded that he had groped about the head of my bunk instead of the foot; so he was sent down again, with repeated instructions and descriptions. This time he brought up the keys, which were in their bags. It appears that the mattress of the bunk had been carried upward by its buoyancy and had lifted the bags off the hooks. They were found just on top of the mattress, immediately above the hooks on which they had hung. The navigator, who was also ordnance officer, found that the key of every magazine and shell-room, including all spare keys, had been recovered. My relief was very great.

The next effort was to recover my private correspondence with General Lee, which I kept in a locked drawer in the bureau of my state-room. There would have been no harm, perhaps, in exhibiting these letters, but they contained an offhand correspondence; therefore I preferred that they should be recovered. In groping within this drawer, the diver got all he could take in his hands, for he could see nothing. He came to the surface with the papers, my watch, and my decoration of the Red Eagle of Prussia, which had been given me by Emperor William I of Germany, in consideration of my deep-sea inventions, and a gold medal which had been awarded me by the International Fisheries Exhibition in London for the same inventions. The latter had been exhibited by the United States Commission of Fish and Fisheries, or by the Smithsonian Institution, I have forgotten which. The decoration and the watch had associations not without public relation, and I may be pardoned for a digression, to state why they were of special value to me.

The decoration had been conferred on me after six years' hard work in deep-sea invention and investigation, in which I had given the United States government freely all of my inventions. The first tangible recognition that I had received from any source came from the Emperor of Germany, through the German minister, the State Department, and the Navy Department. The Constitution of the United States requires an act of Congress to enable any United States official to receive a decoration or present from any foreign potentate or power. The first public recognition of my work from my own country was a prompt adverse report from the Senate Committee on Foreign Affairs when the question

The Wrecking and the Inquiry

of allowing me to accept the decoration came up in Congress. This was disappointing, especially as the German minister expressed concern; but, through the courtesy of certain senators, the report was referred back to the committee for reconsideration, and I was finally allowed to receive the decoration. The inventions were developed between the years 1874 and 1878, while I had command of the Coast Survey steamer *Blake*, engaged in deep-sea exploration for my own government, part of the time in association with Professor Alexander Agassiz. The *Blake* was afterward exhibited at the Columbian Exposition at Chicago. The principal part of her outfit on that occasion consisted of my inventions or adaptations. The judge in the class under which the inventions came was Captain Concas[1] of the Spanish navy, whom I had never met. He recommended me personally for an award, but when the question was considered by the authorities at the exposition, it was decided that the government, being the exhibitor, should get the award, and the government got it. A high privilege of the nautical man, high or low, here or there, is to grumble away his grievances. Since it can probably be shown that my inven-

---

[1] Captain Concas, it will be remembered, was in command of the *Infanta Maria Teresa* in the naval action off Santiago de Cuba.

tions or fittings have saved the United States government more than one hundred thousand dollars, assuming that it would have done, without their help, the same work that it has done with them, it may be claimed that I am exercising my privilege with more than ordinary foundation.

My watch was not without marine history. It had been down in salt water three times: once in Japan, many years ago, and the second time in Cuba, about 1878. The second submergence occurred while I was in command of the Coast Survey steamer *Blake*, engaged in deep-sea exploration in the Gulf of Mexico. Professor Alexander Agassiz was then associated with me for the dredging work which was made a specialty that season. The *Blake* had been to Havana, where she had obtained authority from the captain-general to enter Bahia Honda, about forty-five miles west of Havana. It was not a port of entry. We were informed that directions had been given there to afford us every facility for the prosecution of the scientific work in which we were engaged. One afternoon, while off Bahia Honda, our steel dredge-rope fouled in the machinery and needed splicing, a tedious operation, suggesting an anchorage in port. It was also desired to enter for the purpose of

GROUP OF PETTY OFFICERS ON BOARD THE "MAINE."
The two whose names are added above were saved. At least eleven were killed. The others were not attached to the ship at the time of the explosion.

The Wrecking and the Inquiry

obtaining, if possible, a pilot for the Colorado Reefs, to the westward, reefs which have never been properly surveyed. During the day a Spanish official boarded the *Blake*, acting under directions from Havana, and offered to send us a pilot if we should make a signal for that purpose. When it was decided, rather late in the day, to enter the port, the usual signal for a pilot was made. I could not enter without one, because it was too late in the day to discern the channel clearly from the deck, and I had not the necessary charts and books to inform myself.

A boat under the Spanish flag put off promptly from the Spanish fort, and one of her people presented himself as a pilot. In several minutes after his acceptance he grounded the *Blake* badly, on hard rock bottom, half a mile from shore. A few days afterward a gale came on, and the sea made quickly. We were on a lee shore. Officers and crew, excepting a few of us, were landed at the fort. By eight o'clock the sea was beating heavily against the vessel, and she was pounding hard. The pipes in her engine-room began to crack, and there were indications that she would soon go to pieces. I then ordered that the joint of the Kingston valve be opened, that the water might enter the vessel and fill her up to the outside level.

The "Maine"

She was flooded, and her buoyancy being destroyed thereby, she ceased to pound. Then the rest of us abandoned her for the night. Afterward, during the efforts to get her off, a tugboat from Havana, with an immense hawser made fast to the *Blake*, suddenly surged on the hawser. It flew violently upward and quivered under great tension. I was then almost exactly under it. Believing that when the reaction took place and the hawser descended it would kill me and the single man in the dinghy with me, I shouted to him to get overboard. I myself jumped, with the result that my watch was filled with salt water. The *Blake* was afterward floated, and completed a good season's work. The Spaniards had not thought that we could save the vessel. I asked the superintendent of the Coast Survey for a board or court of inquiry. He replied by cable: "No court of inquiry necessary: hearty thanks and congratulations to yourself, officers, and crew for saving the *Blake*."

It was ascertained that the man sent to pilot us in was a common boatman who had only recently arrived from Santiago de Cuba. He knew absolutely nothing of the channel into Bahia Honda. There were certain vexatious incidents connected with that case. The day after the

The Wrecking and the Inquiry

grounding of the *Blake*, a Spanish naval officer, under orders from the Spanish admiral at Havana, arrived at Bahia Honda on board an American merchant steamer, to make offer of assistance. He was informed of our needs, whereupon he returned to Havana. Nothing at all was done by the Spaniards for our relief until Professor Agassiz went to Havana, when, by extraordinary efforts, he managed to get from the navy-yard an anchor and a hawser. No apology or expression of regret for the grounding of the vessel was received, and on the night of the grounding, when I sent an officer ashore to a telegraph office about six miles away, with a report to the superintendent of the Coast Survey that I had been grounded by a pilot, the censorship was applied to my despatch, and I was not allowed to telegraph that there was a pilot on board, for the reason, as given by the Spaniards, that the man sent was not a pilot. On that occasion, also, there was an exhibition of courtesy. The governor of the province visited the ship, and the captain of the port, or the equivalent official, was almost constant in his attendance on the vessel during the daytime, as a matter of either courtesy or observation. He gave us no assistance except to advise us to get ashore as soon as a gale came on. He said the sea would make

The "Maine"

very rapidly. It is only fair to say that there was a fête at Havana during the period stated, which may have interfered with measures which otherwise might have been taken for our relief. A short time thereafter a Spanish man-of-war met with disaster off our coast; her people, as I now remember the case, were rescued by a United States revenue cutter, and were carefully cared for on board the receiving-ship at New York.

I had in view the Bahia Honda censorship when I wrote "suspend *opinion*," instead of "suspend *judgment*," in my Havana despatch.

When I took command of the *St. Paul*, engaged in the war between Spain and the United States, I thought it unwise again to risk that watch in Cuban waters, so I left it at home, and during the war wore a very cheap one. This recital is hardly pertinent to my narrative of the loss of the *Maine*, but I have many times been asked to state the circumstances connected with the submergence of my watch the first time in Cuba.

To return to the wreck of the *Maine*, I find that, up to the night of February 21, one hundred and forty-three bodies had been recovered from the wreck and the harbor. On this day Congress passed a joint resolution appropriating two

REVOLVER-DRILL ON THE STARBOARD SUPERSTRUCTURE OF THE "MAINE." MOST OF THESE MEN WERE LOST.

The Wrecking and the Inquiry

hundred thousand dollars for wrecking purposes on the *Maine*. The terms of the joint resolution were as follows:

> That the Secretary of the Navy be and he is hereby authorized to engage the services of a wrecking company or companies having proper facilities for the prompt and efficient performance of submarine work for the purpose of recovering the remains of officers and men lost on the United States steamer *Maine*, and of saving the vessel or such parts thereof, and so much of her stores, guns, material and equipment, fittings and appurtenances, as may be practicable; and for this purpose the sum of two hundred thousand dollars, or so much thereof as may be necessary, is hereby appropriated and made immediately available.

With this the following amendment was incorporated:

> And for the transportation and burial of the remains of the officers and men, so far as possible.

The Navy Department having signed contracts with the Merritt & Chapman Wrecking Company of New York, and the Boston Towboat Company, the wrecking-tug *Right Arm*, belonging to the former company, left Key West for Havana. The contract with the companies put them under my directions as to the kind of work to be done. They were required to work at the recovery of bodies as well as to engage in wrecking the vessel. The tug *Right Arm*, Captain McGee, arrived at Havana on the 23d and began operations on the 24th. She did not remain long. Thereafter the following vessels were employed on the *Maine:* the steam-tug *T. J. Merritt*, the sea-barge *F. R. Sharp*, and the floating derrick *Chief*, all for the New York company, and the steam-tug *Underwriter* and barge *Lone Star*, for the Boston company. The wrecking work on the part of the contractors was in charge of Captain F. R. Sharp, an expert wrecker. During these days we were often shocked by the sight of vultures flying over the wreck or resting on the frames projecting from the ruins of the central superstructure. I sent the following telegram to the Navy Department on the night of the 24th:

Wrecking-tug *Right Arm* arrived yesterday. Begins work to-day. Much encumbering metal must be blasted away in detail. Navy divers down aft seven days, forward four days. Bodies of Jenkins and Merritt not found. Two unidentified bodies of crew found yesterday.

After-compartments filled with detached, broken, and buoyant furniture and fittings; mud and confusion. Spanish authorities continue offers of assistance, and care for wounded and dead. Everything that goes from wreck to United States should be disinfected. Wrecking company should provide for this.

Surgeon of *Maine*, after consultation with others, recom-

The Wrecking and the Inquiry

mended that all bedding and clothing should be abandoned. Might go to acclimated poor. Useless fittings and equipment might be towed to sea and thrown overboard.

Will take all immediate responsibility, but invite department's wishes. Shall old metal of superstructure and the like be saved? Friends of dead should understand that we are in the tropics. Chaplain Chidwick charged with all matters relative to dead. His conduct is beyond praise.

Don't know what reports are being printed, but the intensely active representatives of press here have been very considerate of me and my position.[1]

The Secretary of the Navy approved my recommendations and authorized me to use my own judgment.

United States Senator Redfield Proctor arrived at Havana on board the *Olivette*, from Key West, on the 26th. I met him frequently during his visit, which was wholly occupied in a personal investigation of the condition of affairs in the island. His speech in the Senate relative to Cuban affairs is well remembered for its great effect on the public mind in the United States. Afterward a party of United States senators and members of Congress visited Havana on board a private yacht, with the same object in view as that which inspired the visit of Senator Proctor. This party consisted of Senator Money of Mis-

---

[1] I believe the last paragraph was written in response to a telegram from the Secretary of the Navy in relation to certain publications purporting to give information emanating from me.

sissippi, Senator Thurston of Nebraska, Representative Cummings of New York, and Representative W. A. Smith of Michigan. They were accompanied by other gentlemen and by several ladies, including Mrs. Thurston. The party soon left for Matanzas, to see the condition of things in the neighborhood of that city. We were greatly shocked to learn that Mrs. Thurston, who had visited the *Montgomery* apparently in good health and spirits while in Havana, had died suddenly on board the yacht in the harbor of Matanzas.

During this period the *Bache* was occasionally carrying wounded to Tortugas. The slow recovery of bodies and the organization of our work made it possible by the 28th to send bodies to Key West for burial, and the *Bache* was employed for this sad service. On the 28th the *Bache* left for Tortugas with five wounded men. They were sent to Tortugas to forestall a quarantine at Key West because of the unfavorable reputation of the Havana hospitals. On this trip she carried one unrecognized body to Key West for burial. This was the first body that was buried in our own soil.

On March 2, the day after the arrival of the *Vizcaya*, the Spanish divers made their first descent. They continued their work almost daily

SPANISH DIVERS AT WORK OUTSIDE THE WRECK OF THE "MAINE."

The Wrecking and the Inquiry

until March 19, commonly with only one diver down at a time, but occasionally with two. Their time spent in diving aggregated two days twenty-two hours and ten minutes for a single diver — a fair amount, but not comparable with the time occupied by the United States divers. The Spaniards worked chiefly from a position outside the ship, forward on the starboard side. To us it appeared that they devoted considerable attention to the locality outside of the *Maine*. Their operations were quite distinct from ours; each party pursued its own course undisturbed by the other.

The naval divers of the United States who gave testimony were Gunner Charles Morgan of the *New York*, Chief Gunner's Mate Andrew Olsen and Gunner's Mate Thomas Smith of the *Iowa*, Gunner's Mates W. H. F. Schluter and Carl Rundquist of the *New York*, and Seaman Martin Redan of the *Maine*. For the wrecking companies the divers were Captain John Haggerty and William H. Dwyer, both men of great diving experience. I think nearly all the young officers of the line of the navy associated with me at that time begged to be allowed to dive in armor at times when points involving close decision came up. Ensign Charles S. Bookwalter, Ensign Powelson, and Naval Cadet Holden certainly offered their services, and I think Naval Cadet Cluverius also.

I found Captain Pedro del Peral of the Spanish navy, who was in charge of the Spanish investigation, a highly intelligent and most agreeable officer. His relations with me were always pleasant. It did not appear to us United States officers that the Spanish diving work was as thorough as our own. Doubtless the Spanish commission or court of instruction had its own way of doing things, without respect to our views; nevertheless, the Spanish official investigation lacked the scientific and sifting quality that characterized that of the United States.[1]

The United States court of inquiry took up thoroughly the question of explosion from the interior, and was unsparing of individuals in its investigation. It endeavored to ascertain if mistakes had been made, if there was laxity in any direction pointing to culpability on the part of those on board, and if the conditions of duty, stowage, and routine favored an interior explosion. It would have been very gratifying to me, and doubtless to other survivors of the *Maine*, had the Spanish commission made an investiga-

---

[1] The report of the Spanish court is contained in Document No. 405, House of Representatives, Fifty-fifth Congress, Second Session. Its final findings are given in Appendix F.

The Wrecking and the Inquiry

tion of the same searching and exhaustive character relative to matters exterior to the vessel. On the Spanish side we find no investigation as to the existence or non-existence of mines in the harbor, nor as to the possible existence at Havana of explosives or torpedoes that could have been used against the *Maine*. Although the advantages for investigation as to interior causes were on the American side, they were as decidedly on the Spanish side in all that related to matters exterior to the *Maine*.

The Spanish report as published in the document already referred to was submitted to the United States government by the Spanish minister at Washington as the "full testimony in the inquiry." On page 596 of the document is published a preliminary report relating to the cause of the disaster. The preliminary report is dated in the printed United States document April 20, which is an error, my authority for this statement being the Department of State. The actual date of the report is February 20, only five days after the explosion, and one day before the United States court met at Havana. The report finds, "although in reserved character," that the explosion was not caused by an accident exterior to the *Maine*.

The "Maine"

The following is a copy of the report:

Thinking it proper, in view of the importance of the unfortunate accident occurring to the North American ironclad *Maine*, to anticipate, although in reserved character, something of that which in brief will form part of the opinion of the fiscal [attorney-general] upon that which I undersign, and in case your Excellency should think it opportune and proper to inform the government of her Majesty thereof, I have the honor to express to your Excellency that from the judicial proceedings up to to-day in the matter, with the investigation with which you charged me immediately after the occurrence of the catastrophe, it is disclosed in conclusive manner that the explosion was not caused by any accident exterior to the boat, and that the aid lent by our officers and marines was brought about with true interest by all and in a heroic manner by some.

It alone remains to terminate this despatch that when the court can hear the testimony of the crew of the *Maine*, and make investigation of its interior, some light may be attained to deduce, if it is possible, the true original cause of the event produced in the interior of the ship. God guard your Excellency many years.

At a certain stage after the court had begun its investigation it appeared to the members, and also to General Lee, that there was no longer any objection to the Spanish authorities beginning their independent investigation by means of diving in and about the wreck. It was suggested that I invite the Spanish authorities to begin operations. I declined, although

A VIEW OF THE SMOKING WRECK OF THE "MAINE," TAKEN EARLY IN THE MORNING AFTER THE EXPLOSION.
From a photograph by Mr. George Bronson Rea.

willing to have them proceed. At that time I had full control of the *Maine*, and remembered that the Spanish authorities had previously assumed a dictatorial position in reference to my command. I therefore declined to move in the matter except with the express authorization of the United States government, thinking it a very essential point that no access to the *Maine* should be given in advance of that authorization. The question was referred, as desired; the authority was given me, and I was content, because it was my sincere belief that the Spanish government had at least a strong moral right to investigate the wreck of the *Maine*.

The Spanish investigation was ordered immediately after the explosion. In fact, the Spanish commission began taking testimony one hour thereafter, the first witness being Ensign Manuel Tamayo, who was officer of the deck of the *Alfonso XII* at the time of the explosion. In my conversation with Spanish officers, in which frankness seemed to be the rule, they placed great stress on certain phenomena attending the explosion, such, for example, as the column of flame or water thrown up, the concussion on shore, and on board the ships in the harbor, the waves propagated in the harbor, the apparent absence of dead fish in the water after the explosion, etc., all of which were very proper to be considered for what they were worth. The United States court of inquiry took up these points also, but the general tenor of its investigation was much more rigid. As to the number of fish killed, it was said by certain people that there were not many fish in the harbor of Havana, even in the daytime, and that at night they took to the sea outside; but it is believed that no great weight was attached to this statement on our side. Our own officers knew that, of the many fish commonly thrown to the surface by the explosion of a submarine torpedo, most of them are merely stunned, and if left undisturbed will swim away in a short time.

As already said, General Blanco had been promised that no American newspaper correspondents should be permitted to enter into any investigation of the *Maine*. His request was hardly necessary, but I saw that his wishes were fulfilled. The ubiquitous American newspaper correspondent could not be denied, however. It caused our officers some amusement to see occasionally a certain newspaper correspondent sitting in the stern of the Spanish divers' boat while it was working on the wreck. I made no objection. The incident put me on the better side of any contention that might arise, and it was not believed that the correspondent would gather much information worthy of publication. This particular correspondent afterward said that the Spaniards knew that he was an American, but allowed him to make his visits, believing that he was actuated only by a purely scientific spirit of observation.

It was fortunate that Ensign Wilfred V. N. Powelson was serving on board the *Fern*. His services to the court were of inestimable value. Ensign Powelson had been the head man of his class at the Naval Academy. After graduation and a short service in the line he began a course of study in naval architecture at Glasgow, Scotland, with a view of entering the Corps of Naval Constructors. At the end of the first year in Glasgow he decided to remain a line officer, whereupon he was allowed to discontinue the course and resume his previous duties. Naval architecture and naval construction were taught at the United States Naval Academy in fair degree also. The scientific tendencies of Ensign Powelson and his studies at the Naval Academy and at Glasgow gave him a special fitness for the investigation of the wreck, which he pursued with unceasing interest and care. Under the direction of Lieutenant-Commander Wainwright, he ordered, in the largest degree, the details of the operations of the divers. His system was admirable. He would have the divers measure different parts of the submerged structural features of the vessel, and, in case of doubt, would have more than one diver take measurements of the same parts. Then he would refer these measurements to the detailed drawings of the *Maine*, which we had in abundance. In this way he would show beyond question the precise position that the several parts had occupied in the structure of the *Maine*. To illustrate his methods: If a piece of the bottom plating of the vessel had a certain longitudinal measurement between frames, he would show that the piece must have come between certain frames. By measuring the transverse width of the plate and other dimensions, he would demonstrate that it could have come only from a certain position between those frames. If there was a manhole plate, he would show that it could be only a certain manhole plate, the precise position of which when intact he could refer to the drawing. He would question the divers and formulate their reports. Then his testimony before the court, verified by the testimony of the divers, would go on the record of the court for consideration. Through this careful method of investigation it was ascertained that at Frame 17 the bottom plating of the ship had been forced up

LIEUTENANT-COMMANDER RICHARD WAINRIGHT,
EXECUTIVE OFFICER OF THE "MAINE."

The Wrecking and the Inquiry

so as to be four feet above the surface of the water, or thirty-four feet above where it would have been had the ship sunk uninjured; also that the vertical and flat keels had been similarly forced up in a way that could have been produced only by a mine exploded under the bottom of the ship.

When the court had concluded its labors at Havana, I desired to relieve myself of the neutral condition of mind in which I had thought it proper to continue while the court's investigation proceeded. There was, naturally, no indication from the court as to the character of its findings. I invited Ensign Powelson to formulate his views as to the initial seat of the explosion, in a written report to me. His testimony before the court of inquiry had been a recitation of details. His report to me embraces his own reasoning and conclusions, and is given in Appendix E. I wished the truth and nothing but the truth, and I wished it as disconnected from my own suspicions and prejudices. Ensign Powelson's report in connection with the testimony of others before the court convinced me that I could accept my own views which had been allowed to lie dormant. I never believed any other theory than that the *Maine* was blown up from the outside, but I should have surrendered my view to an adverse finding of the court based on adequate ground. The murder of two hundred and fifty sleeping and unoffending men is too great a crime to charge against any man's soul without proof.

The court investigated first the probability of an interior cause. The discipline of the ship and the precautions taken against explosion from the inside, whether fortuitous or as the result of treachery, were subjected to careful inquiry. The testimony, as connected with a possible interior cause, apparently reduced that aspect of the case to the consideration of a single "pocket" coal-bunker on the port side, adjoining the six-inch reserve magazine. The counterpart of this bunker on the starboard side was in use on the day of the explosion, and was therefore outside the realm of suspicion. Only the two aftermost boilers of the ship were in use. The pocket-bunker which was most seriously in question had been full of coal in a stable condition for three months. Its temperature had been regularly taken, and the temperatures of the magazine adjoining it had been taken every day and recorded. The bunkers were provided with electrical alarms of unusual sensitiveness, the indications of which were recorded on a ringing annunciator near my cabin door. It so hap-

The Wrecking and the Inquiry

pened, fortunately for the investigation, that the bunker in question was the most exposed on its outer surface of all in the ship. It was exposed on three sides. On the deck above the magazine it formed three sides of a passageway which was traversed many times a day, and the hands of officers and men were placed on the sides of the bunker, unconsciously, in passing that way. Certain lounging-places for the crew were bounded by the walls of that bunker. Its temperature was taken on the day of the explosion. In the testimony before the court there seemed to arise hardly a suspicion in any direction pointing to an interior cause, further than that this bunker was full of coal and was, in fact, next to a magazine. A strong point was the fact that the boilers next those forward bunkers had not been active for three months. On the contrary, there were many facts developed which conspired to indicate that the primary explosion was outside the vessel.

No American, so far as I know, appeared before the Spanish court or commission, and no Spaniard before the American court; but a foreigner, a resident of Havana for many years, gave testimony before the latter. According to his own account, this witness must have held the opinion that he was in a country where distaste-

The "Maine"

ful people were likely to be murderously dealt with. It is not clear, therefore, why he chose to testify and run into danger. I formed the suspicion that he was a detective, and gave no credence to his unsupported testimony; I doubt that anybody else did.

It seems unlikely that the agency which produced the explosion of the *Maine* will always remain unknown. It will be sought with more persistency than has been brought to bear on the investigation of the first landing-place of Columbus, the final resting-place of his remains, or the identity of the "iron mask."

The court of inquiry was obliged to meet in turn both at Key West and Havana, because the *Maine's* people had been distributed. The *Mangrove*, with the court aboard, left Havana for Key West on February 26, returned on March 5, and left finally on March 15. It completed its report at Key West on March 21, one month after its first sitting at Havana. Its findings are given in Appendix C. On March 28 its report was transmitted to Congress in a message from the President of the United States, which is given in Appendix D. The rapid movement of events toward war with Spain after the reception by Congress of the President's message is a matter of current history; so is the downfall

LIEUTENANT JOHN J. BLANDIN,
Who survived the explosion, but who died on July 16, 1898.

The Wrecking and the Inquiry

of Spanish colonization through the operations of the United States army and navy.

After the court had completed its work at Havana, the wrecking operations on the *Maine*, under the direction of Lieutenant-Commander Wainwright (who had as an assistant Naval Cadet Cluverius, a very able and conscientious young officer), became the event of chief interest. Nearly, if not quite, all her guns were recovered, but not those in the turrets. The breech-blocks of the after-turret guns were recovered and saved. I had recommended that bags of crystal acid be put into the chambers of the turret guns to eat away the tubes, but I doubt that this was done.

The forward half of the *Maine* was distorted and disintegrated beyond repair. She was hardly worth raising for any practical purpose whatever, but it took time completely to develop this conclusion. Toward the last, the wrecking force having removed all the parts above water that could be detached by ordinary means, Captain Sharp desired to use dynamite, in small charges or in the form of tape, to blast away connecting parts in detail. He requested me to apply to the Spanish officials for authority to import about two hundred pounds of dynamite. I made known his wishes to General Lee, who reported them to the Spanish authorities, with a request from me that a place be named where the dynamite might be kept. General Blanco bluntly, even contentiously, refused the request. This virtually reduced the wrecking work to the recovery of armament, equipment, and fittings. The Navy Department then informed me that it did not approve the use of dynamite. The situation, by that time, was strained beyond relief.

On March 26 all of the *Maine's* officers except Lieutenant-Commander Wainwright were detached and left Havana for Key West by the *Olivette*, Wainwright remaining behind to represent the government in connection with the wrecking companies. General Lee, many American newspaper correspondents, and other gentlemen, and a few ladies, came on board to see us off. After a time we were invited into the dining-cabin. Attention was soon demanded by General Lee, who made a short and touching address to me in which he showed much feeling. He and I had worked together so completely in unison during the stress of the great disaster that the breaking of the bond could not but be felt deeply by both of us. He then presented to me, in behalf of the American press correspondents in Havana, a beautiful floral piece which had been brought on board. I replied in a short

The Wrecking and the Inquiry

address, in which I returned thanks and expressed my appreciation of the kind forbearance that had been shown to me by the gentlemen of the press in Havana. The parting was a solemn one to me, and, I think, to all present. The small American colony which had held together in close sympathy during the whole trying period following the loss of the *Maine* was now breaking up; and the interruption of friendly relations with Spain was at hand. I was completely taken by surprise by this cordial demonstration of the newspaper correspondents. Since I had been able to do but little for them in their official characters, it pleased me greatly that I had nevertheless won their private regard. I find that it takes a strong effort of moral courage to refer in this way to gentlemen of the press, — one's motive may so easily be misconstrued, — but to one who will try to fancy himself in the position that I occupied at Havana, the gratification that I have expressed, and my desire to express it far more strongly, should be apparent.

On leaving Havana, I disliked exceedingly to have Lieutenant-Commander Wainwright remain behind. My first official act afterward, when I arrived at the Navy Department, was to recommend that he be relieved. He had had

The "Maine"

a long and difficult tour of duty in connection with the wreck, during which he had borne up nobly. On the day after our departure from Key West, the *Bache* returned to Havana harbor, with Captain Chadwick, as senior member of a board, in association with Lieutenant-Commanders Cowles and Wainwright, to determine the final disposition that should be made of the wreck. They soon after reported adversely as to further measures. Wrecking operations were therefore abandoned. Lieutenant-Commander Wainwright left Havana about April 5; General Lee and the American citizens, as a body, on April 9. General Lee left on board the *Fern*, with Lieutenant-Commander Cowles. As the *Fern* steamed out of the harbor derisive whistles from people on shore were heard.

My duties at Havana were confined so specifically to certain features of the situation that I was not personally cognizant of much that was going on about me, and concerning which I regret that I am not better informed. For example, there was much kindness shown by kind-hearted people to our men at the hospital at Havana. I remember especially the attentions of Sister Mary Wilberforce and Mr. Charles Carbonell. The Spanish surgeon in charge of the hospital at Havana should not be forgotten;

Naval Cadet David F. Boyd, Jr.   Paymaster Charles M. Ray.   Pay-clerk Brent McCarthy.
Surgeon Lucien G. Heneberger.   Lieut. Albertus W. Catlin.   Gunner Joseph Hill.
Carpenter George Helms.

The Wrecking and the Inquiry

every report that came to me from the hospital showed that he gave our men the very best care to be had in that institution. The report of the Spanish Court of Instruction shows that helpfulness was wide-spread among the Spaniards. At Key West the wounded were cared for in the hospital at the army barracks and in the marine hospital near the fort. The citizens of Key West were very attentive to the wounded men.

On arriving in Washington, I reported to the Hon. John D. Long, Secretary of the Navy. The Secretary took me to the Executive Mansion, where he presented me to President McKinley, who greeted me cordially and with kind words. My immediate connection with the disaster to the *Maine* may be said to have ended on the night of April 2, when a reception was given to me at the Arlington Hotel in Washington by the National Geographical Society, of which I am a member; it was under the direction of the president of the society, Professor Alexander Graham Bell, assisted by some of his associates. The reception was attended by the President of the United States, the Vice-President, the Secretary of the Navy, and many distinguished gentlemen, official and private, in Washington at that time. Ladies were present in equal number with the men. I greatly regretted that, through force of adverse circumstances, I was the only representative of the *Maine* present. Perhaps no more distinctive personal honor has ever been paid by the President of the United States to a naval officer than was shown me that night. My only regret was that it could not, in some way, have found a place on the files of the Navy Department. An officer whose life is spent in the naval service is keenly alive in all matters affecting his official record.

I was deeply disappointed that there was no battle-ship the command of which was vacant. I had hoped for an immediate command of that nature, some vessel at least as large as the *Maine*, as a mark of the continued confidence of the government, officially and publicly expressed. I mentioned my regret to the President and the Secretary of the Navy. The day after the reception I told the Secretary of the Navy that I withdrew all question as to the size of a command, and was desirous of accepting any command where I could be of service. With great consideration, the secretary soon gave me the command of the auxiliary cruiser *St. Paul*, which was probably the largest man-of-war ever commanded by any-

The Wrecking and the Inquiry

body. Her displacement was sixteen thousand tons, or four thousand tons more than that of our largest battle-ship, the *Iowa*. She was under complete man-of-war organization.

As might have been expected, the surviving officers and crew of the *Maine* were much scattered after their formal detachment from that vessel. Members of the crew, as a rule, were distributed among vessels at Key West. Lieutenant-Commander Wainwright was given command of the *Gloucester*. He did fine service with that vessel on the south side of Cuba, and, later, on the south side of Porto Rico. The action of the *Gloucester* with the torpedo-boat destroyers *Pluton* and *Furor* is well remembered. Lieutenant Holman was ordered to the torpedo-station at Newport; Lieutenant Hood was first given command of the *Hornet*, and later was attached to the *Topeka;* Lieutenant Jungen was given command of the *Wampatuck;* Lieutenant Blow commanded the *Potomac*, and later was attached to the *Vulcan;* Lieutenant Blandin was attached to the Bureau of Equipment, Navy Department: he died on July 16; Naval Cadets Holden and Cluverius were attached to the *Scorpion* under the command of Lieutenant-Commander Marix; Naval Cadet Bronson was attached first to the *Scorpion* and then to the *Amphitrite;* Naval Cadet Boyd was attached first to the flagship *New York* and later to the *Cushing.*

Staff-officers were ordered to service as follow: Dr. Heneberger to the *St. Paul*, under my command; Paymaster Ray in charge of the navy pay-office, at Baltimore; Chief Engineer Howell to the *Newark;* Passed Assistant Engineer Bowers to the New York navy-yard; Assistant Engineer Morris to the *Columbia;* Naval Cadet Washington to the *New Orleans;* Naval Cadet Crenshaw to the *San Francisco*, and at the time of this writing he is on board the *Texas* under my command; Chaplain Chidwick to the *Cincinnati;* First Lieutenant of Marines Catlin to the *St. Louis;* Boatswain Larkin to the League Island navy-yard; Gunner Hill to the New York navy-yard; Carpenter Helm to the receiving-ship *Vermont;* Pay-Clerk McCarthy to the *Columbia;* Sergeant Anthony was transferred to the *Detroit*, where he served during the war.

While in Washington I was directed to appear before the Committees on Foreign Relations in the Senate and the House. The committees questioned me freely on points tending to amplify the investigation of the court of inquiry. One of the committees desired to be informed, substantially, if I could attribute the loss of the

Naval Cadet Arthur Crenshaw.   Boatswain Francis E. Larkin.   Naval Cadet Pope Washington.
Passed Asst. Eng. Frederic C. Bowers.   Chaplain John P. Chidwick.   Asst. Eng. John R. Morris.
Chief Eng. Charles P. Howell.

The Wrecking and the Inquiry

Maine to any special mechanical agency or to any person or persons. I replied that I had no knowledge that would enable me to form a judgment in those particulars. I was then pressed, formally and informally, as to possibilities instead of probabilities. When the investigation took a hypothetical character, I explained a mechanical means whereby the *Maine* could have been blown up, and referred to persons who were in a position which would have enabled them to blow her up had they been so inclined. It was well understood on both sides that no charge was made, since no evidence existed. The plan shown was of my own conception. The committee was informed that the watering population of Havana was Spanish, not Cuban; also that there were many Spaniards in Havana who presumably had more or less knowledge of torpedoes and submarine mines, and who could have blown up the *Maine* had they so desired. This personal phase of the investigation was not pleasant to me, because it did not deal with known actualities, but, beyond doubt, the committee was right in pressing the inquiry as far as it deemed necessary. The loss of the *Maine* was not a subject of investigation in which the committee was likely to feel unduly inclined to deference toward any persons whatever.

The "Maine"

The mechanical plan is shown in Fig. 1, on this page. The *Maine*, *A*, swinging in a complete circle around the fixed mooring-buoy, *B*, would have covered progressively every part of the area

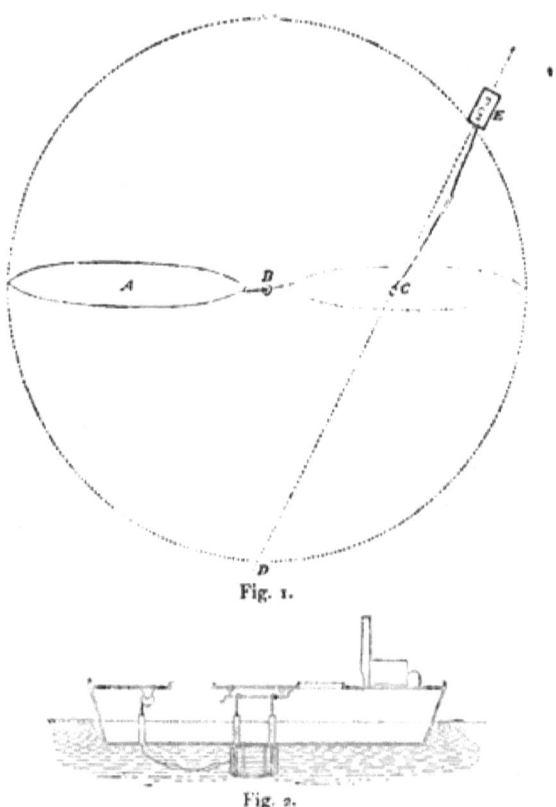

Fig. 1.

Fig. 2.

DIAGRAM SHOWING HOW A MINE MIGHT HAVE BEEN PLACED UNDER THE "MAINE."

bounded by the dotted line shown in the diagram. Therefore at some time during her swing she would have been over a mine planted anywhere in that area as at *C*. To blow her up

The Wrecking and the Inquiry

would have been an easy matter, if a mine could have been so planted without suspicion. It would have been chiefly a question of time to await the favorable moment, and of immunity from suspicion and arrest. Many lighters were moving about in the harbor every day; some passed and repassed the *Maine* in various directions. Could a lighter, taking advantage of this traffic, have proceeded past the *Maine* along any route, as DE, crossing the area of danger, and have dropped a mine without detection? It is believed that she could have succeeded, even though the men on lookout on board the *Maine* had been watching her at the time. The method that I conceive could have been employed was explained by me to Captain Sampson and Commander Converse on board the *Montgomery*. Each, in turn, had been in charge of the Torpedo School at Newport. They admitted that the plan was feasible, and when I pointed to a lighter passing ahead of the *Montgomery*, each admitted that if she were then dropping a mine, according to the plan described, we could not detect her in the act. It was maintained, however, that it would require about twelve persons of different kinds of skill, acting in collusion, to execute the plan in its entirety.

The "Maine"

Fig. 2, page 182, represents my idea of such a lighter and of her procedure. Under a decked lighter of large capacity is slung a mine very large, but so loaded that its specific gravity, as a whole, is only slightly greater than that of the harbor water. Let it weigh, say, one hundred pounds in water. It is slung from a tripping-bar within the lighter, the slings passing through tubes which are let into the bottom of the lighter and extend upward above the level of the outside water. Insulated wires lead forward from the mine and through a similar tube to a reel mounted within the lighter. If a lighter, so prepared, is slowly towed through the water, or preferably driven slowly by a noisy geared engine, of the type seen in Havana, she can drop her mine on ranges, unobserved, as she may choose. The mine being wholly submerged, no wave will be noticed on letting go; there will be no jump of the lighter, any more than would be evident were one of her crew to fall overboard. With a heavy lighter there will be no sudden change of speed; at least, this can be provided against by opening the throttle of the engine wider at the right time. When the mine drops, the electrical wires pay out automatically. The lighter goes alongside a wharf or anchors. She may land her wires, if opportu-

Lieutenant John Hood.   Naval Cadet Jonas H. Holden.   Naval Cadet Watt T. Cluverius.
Lieutenant George P. Blow.   Lieut. George F. W. Holman.   Naval Cadet Amon Bronson, Jr.
                       Lieut. Carl W. Jungen.

nity serves, or at the right moment the explosion is caused electrically on board the lighter. She then leaves her berth, drops her wires elsewhere, and disposes of her fittings.

On board the *Maine* the greatest watchfulness was observed against measures of this kind; not that I believed we were likely to be blown up, but as a proper precaution in a port of unfriendly feeling. On the day of the explosion, or the day before, I caused ten or twelve reports to be made to me concerning a single lighter that passed and repassed the *Maine*. She did not pass within what I may call the area of danger, and she was not of a type to have carried out the plan just set forth.

In dwelling on these problematical matters it should not be thought that it is intended to point to any individual responsibility for the *Maine* disaster. I shall not break my rule of reserve, but, short of personal accusation, investigation of so horrible a disaster may pursue any promising line of thought, even beyond suspicion and into the domain of abstract possibility.

It cannot be doubted that a large number of the people of the United States have refused to relieve Spain of moral responsibility for the loss of the *Maine*. In conversation with many Americans, and, notably, with a distinguished citizen who has held high public office at home as well as high diplomatic office abroad, I have gathered points in what the latter gentleman calls an indictment. Since these points indicate public opinion in considerable degree, it may be of interest to set them forth here, especially as they may have guided public action indirectly through individual activity.

Spain, in respect to Cuba, was not friendly to the United States. Havana was heavily fortified on the sea-front, not against Cuba, but, obviously, against the United States. The *Maine* was not welcome at Havana. Her coming was officially opposed on the ground that it might produce an adverse demonstration. By officials she was treated with outward courtesy; otherwise, she was made to feel that she was unwelcome. She was taken to a special mooring-buoy — a buoy that, according to the testimony given before the United States naval court of inquiry, was apparently reserved for some purpose not known. She was taken to this buoy by an official Spanish pilot, and she was blown up at that buoy by an explosion from the outside. Therefore there must have been a mine under the *Maine's* berth when she entered the harbor, or a mine must have been planted at her berth after her arrival. In either case, the *Maine*

The Wrecking and the Inquiry

should have been protected by the Spanish government. She was not informed of the existence of a mine at her berth, or cautioned in any wise against danger from mines or torpedoes. In her attitude of initial and reiterated friendship, she was powerless to search her mooring-berth. She was obliged to assume a due sense of responsibility on the part of the Spanish authorities. Yet it has not appeared that they took any measures to guard her. Mining plants for harbor defense, and their electrical connections, are always under the express control of governments, and in charge of a few people who alone have the secret of position and control. Therefore responsibility for accident, or worse, is centralized and specific.

At Havana the regulations were severe against the ownership of explosives by private parties. The government rigorously controlled the importation and sale of explosives. It was seemingly impracticable to obtain any large amount of explosives, except through the acquiescence of some official. A knowledge of the secret operation of large mines as against due official vigilance was not likely to be possessed at Havana by private parties acting alone. After the explosion the Spanish authorities endeavored to control access to the *Maine* and to prevent an independent investigation by the United States. Although they

The "Maine"

demanded an investigation of the interior of the *Maine* for themselves, they objected to an exterior investigation by the United States. The Spanish government in Cuba had allowed rioters to go unpunished. The Spanish investigation was superficial and its findings were prejudged by officials. After the explosion there was not a free-handed demonstration that no mines had existed in the harbor of Havana at the *Maine's* berth at the time of the explosion. A general declaration by General Weyler that there were no mines planted during his administration was not acceptable to the people of the United States. The war developed the fact that the Spaniards had mines in large number in Cuba. It was known in the United States that there were mines, planted or unplanted, at Havana.

On April 6 the "Heraldo," the leading and most influential evening paper in Madrid, published a very circumstantial interview with Vice-Admiral Beranger, secretary of the navy in the last Conservative cabinet of Spain. Among other things, he stated that an attack on their island ports was not to be feared, because "Havana, as well as Cienfuegos, Nuevitas, and Santiago are defended by electrical and automobile torpedoes, which can be worked at a great

THE SECOND-CLASS BATTLESHIP "MAINE," BLOWN UP IN HAVANA HARBOR, FEBRUARY 15, 1898.

Copyright, 1897, by C. E. Bolles, Brooklyn, N. Y.

The Wrecking and the Inquiry

distance [have a large radius of action]. Señor Cánovas del Castillo, who did not neglect these things, arranged, in agreement with me, for the shipping to Cuba of one hundred and ninety torpedoes, which are surely located in these ports at present. The transportation and installation of these war machines was in charge of the distinguished torpedoist Señor Chacon." Cánovas, it will be remembered, was assassinated on August 8, 1897.

Notwithstanding the influence on public opinion in the United States flowing from these considerations, the war was officially prosecuted independent of the affair of the *Maine*. Certainly no American is likely to feel more deeply than I in respect to any policy growing out of that great disaster; but it is very gratifying to my national pride that we, as a nation, have been proof against all suspicion and against all argument, short of actual demonstration. We have heard much of the motto, " Remember the *Maine*." If we are satisfied that the *Maine* was blown up from the outside we have a right to remember her with indignation; but without more conclusive evidence than we now have, we are not right if we charge criminality to persons. Therefore I conceive that the motto, " Remem-

The "Maine"

ber the *Maine*," used as a war-cry would not have been justifiable. I should like to make the point here, as I have made it elsewhere, that this great and free country, with its education, good intention, and universal moral influence, may go to war to punish, but not to revenge. Improperly applied, the motto, "Remember the *Maine*," savors too much of revenge, too much of evil for evil; but it may be used in an entirely worthy sense.

During the recent war with Spain about seventy-five men were killed and wounded in the United States navy. Only seventeen were killed. On board the *Maine* two hundred and fifty-two men were killed outright and eight died later — nearly fifteen times as many as were killed in the United States navy by the Spanish land and naval forces during the entire war. In the way that the men of the *Maine* died and suffered there was enough of the heroic to provide a sound foundation for the motto, "Remember the *Maine*."

Let me dismiss the prevailing impression that this motto was used in the United States navy, in the recent war, as a battle-signal. No United States naval vessel entered into action flying the signal, "Remember the *Maine*." I am glad that it can be so stated; yet one may excuse many mistaken expressions in the heat of action.

It may be further stated that the signal was once used in the United States Coast Signal-Service by a signal quartermaster (an enlisted man), who hoisted it from his station when a transport with troops was passing out to sea. In reporting the departure of the transport, as was his duty, the quartermaster added to his message to headquarters the fact that he had displayed the signal. He was severely reprimanded by return message over the wire.

On July 13, when I boarded the wreck of the *Infanta Maria Teresa* as she lay on the rocks of Cuba, with dead men still in her, I believed and said, as I stood there, that although the Spanish vessels had been brought to ruin after full preparation and in fair fight, the greater dignity belonged to the *Maine*, which was lost on the instant and without warning.

A naval commander both idealizes and personifies his ship. When he leaves her — or loses her — he dismisses from his mind the petty vexations of sea life and remembers only the nobler qualities of his shipmates and his ship. I shall always remember the *Maine* with as much pride

The "Maine"

as any commander who is completely satisfied with his command could possibly feel. The officers and men who were lost with the *Maine* were as worthy and true patriots as those we have lost in battle. Their fate was a sadder one. May God be good to them!

APPENDICES

APPENDIX A

TECHNICAL DESCRIPTION OF THE "MAINE"

THE following account of the *Maine* is drawn almost wholly from a paper by Chief Engineer A. W. Morley, U. S. N., printed in the "Journal of the Society of American Engineers," February, 1895, and entitled "Contract Trial of the United States Armored Cruiser [1] *Maine*."

The *Maine*, a twin-screw armored cruiser of about 6650 tons displacement, was built at the navy-yard, New York, from designs furnished by the Bureau of Construction and Repair of the Navy Department, and was the largest vessel built in any of our navy-yards. In external appearance and in arrangement of battery, she resembled the Brazilian ship *Riachuelo;* but she was larger and had thicker armor and heavier guns. The machinery was built by N. F. Palmer, Jr., & Co., the Quintard Iron Works of New York city, from designs furnished by the Bureau of Steam Engineering of the Navy Department, the contract price of the machinery being $735,000. The contract price called for an indicated horse-power of 9000 for the main engines and the air and circulating pump engines, with a pre-

---

[1] See page 6, second paragraph.

Appendix A

mium of one hundred dollars to be paid for each indicated horse-power in excess of the requirement, and a penalty of like amount to be deducted for each horsepower below that amount. Her keel was laid on October 17, 1888, and her hull was launched on November 18, 1890. The contract for the construction of her machinery was signed on April 3, 1889, and the engines erected in the ship and operated on August 31, 1891. An official dock trial was made on July 21 and 22, 1893. She was commissioned September 17, 1895, and left the navy-yard, New York, on November 5, 1895, drawing twenty-two feet one inch forward and twenty-one feet eight inches aft.

The hull was constructed of mild steel, and all of the material used was of domestic manufacture. The outside keel-plate was five eighths of an inch, the inner plate a half-inch, and the vertical keel a half-inch thick. The outer bottom plating was a half-inch thick, with a double sheer-strake; the plating of the inner bottom was five sixteenths of an inch thick. The frames were spaced four feet throughout the length of the double bottom, and three feet at the ends.

She was divided into two hundred and fourteen watertight compartments, and had a double bottom extending from Frame 18 to Frame 67, a distance of one hundred and ninety-six feet, and running up to the shelf for the armor belt. In the wake of the double bottom there were four longitudinals on each side, and under the engines and boilers intermediate longitudinals were introduced.

Technical Description of the "Maine"

There were twenty coal-bunker compartments, ten on each side of the vessel, extending down from the protective deck, with wing bunkers at each end of each fire-room, extending inboard to the fronts of the boilers. The total capacity, in tons of forty-two cubic feet, was eight hundred and twenty-five tons. The bunkers were filled through trunks leading down from the main-deck, delivering directly into the several main compartments and to the wing bunkers, being so arranged that but little trimming of the coal was required until the bunkers were nearly filled.

DIMENSIONS OF HULL

Length between perpendiculars, feet	310
Length over all, feet and inches	324, 4
Beam, extreme, at L. W. L., feet	57
Draft, mean, normal, feet and inches	21, 6
Area immersed midship section, square feet	1,077
Displacement, tons, at 21 feet 6 inches	6,650
Tons per inch	32.32
Center of buoyancy above base-line, feet and inches	12, 3½
Center of buoyancy aft of midship section, feet and inches	2, 11
Center of gravity below C. B., feet and inches	3, 1
Transverse metacenter above C. B., feet	12
Longitudinal metacenter above C. B., feet	324
Coefficient of displacement, prismoidal, feet	0.596
Coefficient of displacement, cylindrical, feet	0.669
Coefficient of midship section, feet	0.878
Coefficient of L. W. L., feet	0.747
Area of L. W. L. plane, square feet	13,560
Wetted surface, square feet	23,770

For a length of one hundred and eighty feet amidships there was a water-line belt of vertical Harveyized steel armor, extending from three feet above to four

Appendix A

feet below the water-line, twelve inches in thickness from the top to one foot below the water-line, whence it tapered to seven inches at the bottom. The wood backing was eight inches thick, and the plating behind this was in two thicknesses of a half-inch each, stiffened by horizontal angle-bars six by three and a half inches, and by plates five sixteenths of an inch thick, worked intercostally between the vertical frames, and connected with them by angle-bars two and a half by two and a half inches.

The bolts for securing the armor were two and two and eight tenths inches in diameter, with nuts and india-rubber cups and washers on the inner ends of the bolts. The wood backing was secured to the skin plating by bolts one and one eighth inches in diameter.

At the forward end of the armor belt there was an athwartship bulkhead of steel six inches in thickness, with the backing generally arranged as for the side armor.

The protective deck, constructed in two layers of one inch each, extended from the armored bulkhead to the after-end of the side armor, whence it sloped below the water-line with a thickness of three inches.

There was an armored conning-tower built of steel, ten inches thick, elliptical in shape, from which an armored tube four and a half inches thick extended down to the armored deck to protect the steering-gear, voice-tubes, electric wires, and connections of the engine-room telegraphs.

There were two revolving turrets, each fitted with two ten-inch breech-loading rifled guns, placed high enough

Technical Description of the "Maine"

to admit of their all being fired simultaneously on a line parallel with the center-line of the ship, each having an unobstructed fire through an angle of 180° on one side, and through an angle of 64° on the opposite side. Each turret had eight inches of Harveyized steel armor, with plate backing, frames, etc. The revolving parts of the turrets, and the spaces for working and loading the guns, were protected by a fixed barbette of mild steel armor twelve inches in thickness, fitted to a wood and steel-plate backing, and secured by bolts and nuts, as described for the side armor. The turrets and guns were worked by hydraulic gear. Besides the turret guns there were six six-inch breech-loading rifles, two mounted forward inside the superstructure-deck firing directly ahead, two abaft the cabins firing directly astern, and one on each side on the central superstructure-deck.

The ten-inch and the six-inch guns could be fired in broadside, throwing a weight of projectile on each side of about twenty-four hundred pounds at one discharge.

The six-inch guns were worked by hand on central-pivot carriages, and were protected by steel shields two inches thick.

The secondary battery consisted of seven six-pounder Driggs-Schroeder rapid-fire guns, four one-pounder Hotchkiss, four one-pounder Driggs-Schroeder, and four machine-guns (Gatling).

There were four tubes for Whitehead torpedoes, two on each side, discharging directly from the berth-deck.

Appendix A

The ship's motive power was supplied by two vertical, inverted-cylinder, direct-acting, triple-expansion engines, in water-tight compartments separated by a fore-and-aft bulkhead. The high-pressure cylinder of each engine was placed aft and the low-pressure cylinder forward, the latter being so arranged that it could be disconnected when working at low power, and the high- and intermediate-pressure cylinders used under economical condition as a compound engine.

The diameter of her cylinders was as follows: high-pressure cylinder, thirty-five and a half inches; intermediate-pressure cylinder, fifty-seven inches; low-pressure cylinder, eighty-eight inches; stroke of all pistons, thirty-six inches.

Her propellers were made of manganese bronze, and were four-bladed twin screws. The diameter of her propellers was fourteen feet six and a half inches, and their pitch, as set on her trial trip, starboard, 16.08 feet; port, 16.114 feet.

She had eight single-ended steel boilers of the horizontal return-fire tube type, with three corrugated furnaces in each boiler and a separate combustion chamber for each furnace. The boilers were placed in two equal groups in two water-tight compartments, with a central fore-and-aft fire-room in each compartment. There was one smoke-pipe, oval in cross-section, for each group of boilers. The boilers had 573.84 square feet of grate surface. She was provided with a force-draft system in each boiler compartment, for which she had two Sturtevant blowers. Located in the after-part

Technical Description of the "Maine"

of the ship, well below the protective deck, was a combined hand-and-steam steering-engine of Williamson Brothers' patent. The steering-engine was capable of putting the helm hard over from amidships in ten seconds when the vessel was making a speed of seventeen knots. It could be operated either at the engine or from the conning-tower, the pilot-house or the bridge. She was provided with steam-capstan and -windlass, excellent distilling apparatus, electric plant for lighting and minor purposes, and with an ice-making plant and, in connection therewith, a cold-storage compartment. For turning the turrets, hoisting ammunition, and loading and working the turret guns, she was provided with a hydraulic pumping plant. Large and small, everything counted, she carried fifteen boats, including two steam-launches or -cutters.

The official trial for horse-power took place on October 17, 1894, in Long Island Sound. The *Maine* left her anchorage off New London Light at 12 M., and proceeded out through the Race, and when on Watch Hill was turned and headed to the westward in order to make as nearly as practicable a straightway run for the four consecutive hours' trial required by the contract.

The trial began at 1:30 P. M., and ended at 5:30. The weather conditions were not very favorable, for throughout the entire run the ship was steaming against a strong head wind and sea, which increased in force to the end of the trial. The ship was remarkably steady,

Appendix A

and at the maximum speed of the engines very little vibration was noticeable.

The speed was very accurately obtained for a portion of the trial, while running over the official measured course laid down for the trial of the *Ericsson*. The average speed for this 25-mile course was 15.95 knots, or, with a mean allowance of 1.5 knots for the strong head wind and tide, 17.45 knots.

APPENDIX B

FOR THE "VIZCAYA'S" SAFETY [1]

LOCAL POLICE AND FEDERAL NAVY TO GUARD THE SPANISH WAR-SHIP

UNUSUAL precautions have been taken by the government authorities and Chief of Police McCullagh to prevent any possibility of any act of violence against the *Vizcaya*. Lieutenant Alexander Sharp, Jr., U. S. N., who is attached to the office of Assistant Secretary [of the Navy] Roosevelt, visited police headquarters at a very early hour yesterday morning, together with Ensign Paine, U. S. N., and Lieutenant J. G. Sobral, naval attaché of the Spanish legation at Washington.

They inquired for Chief McCullagh, but were told that the chief was at home in bed. Captain Vreedenburgh, who was on duty at headquarters Thursday night, was called from his bed, and saw the visitors.

As a result of the visit, Chief McCullagh was communicated with by telephone, and he at once issued orders to all captains of precincts in the Borough of Manhattan to hold their men in reserve.

[1] Extract from the New York "Herald," Saturday, February 19, 1898.

Appendix B

Lieutenant Sharp, Ensign Paine, and Lieutenant Sobral then left, but about ten o'clock in the morning called again, and had an interview with Chief McCullagh lasting for more than an hour. After they had gone, the chief said their visit was to deliver a request by Rear-Admiral Bunce, commandant of the Brooklyn navy-yard, that policemen be detailed to act in conjunction with the navy-yard authorities for protection of the *Vizcaya*.

Chief McCullagh made public this letter, which he sent to the rear-admiral in the morning:

In compliance with your request, I have ordered Captain Elbert O. Smith of this department, who is in command of the steamboat *Patrol*, to furnish a detail of one roundsman and four patrolmen to each tugboat assigned by you to patrol the waters of New York harbor in the vicinity of the Spanish battle-ship *Vizcaya*.

I have arranged with Ensign Paine to establish tours of patrol duty around the vessel above named, as follows: Two tugs to patrol in the vicinity for eight hours, to be relieved by two tugs from the harbor, these to be relieved in turn by two steam-launches from the Police Department, thus establishing a patrol system during the entire twenty-four hours, the men assigned to such service doing tours of eight hours on and sixteen hours off; such a force of marines to be supplied to each boat as in your judgment is necessary.

Chief McCullagh to-day told me his letter to Rear-Admiral Bunce gave all the explanation concerning Lieutenant Sharp's visit that he cared to give out at present.

"The detail of police," he said, "will be under

For the "Vizcaya's" Safety

command of Captain Elbert O. Smith of the harbor police, who will have sixty-seven men assigned to him for this duty. The police steamboat *Patrol* and six police launches will be available for patrol duty, and will work together with the force from the navy-yard.

"I do not believe, however, that there will be any necessity for the use of the police nor for the force that is to be detailed from the navy-yard for patrol duty. The *Vizcaya* will be perfectly safe in New York harbor, and the steps which are being taken by the government and the Police Department are simply precautionary.

"The patrol will be kept up every hour of the day and night while the Spanish man-of-war is in this port, and no craft of any description whatsoever will be permitted to approach her unless its mission is fully explained to the officer in command of the patrol. Just how close the picket-lines around the war-ship will be drawn is a matter that will be determined by the navy-yard authorities."

Chief McCullagh rescinded in the afternoon the order directing all the police reserves on duty. He declined to make any explanation why he had ordered the reserves on duty or why he had rescinded the order.

Lieutenant Sharp and his companions visited police headquarters in Jersey City, where they saw Chief Murphy and told him the police of his city might be asked to coöperate with the New York police.

Appendix B

Police Captain Smith had his men in readiness all day at the quarters of the harbor police, on Pier A, waiting for word of the *Vizcaya* being sighted. When word came that she had been sighted off Point Pleasant, New Jersey, he started down the bay in the steamboat *Patrol*, accompanied by several launches.

APPENDIX C

FULL FINDINGS OF THE UNITED STATES COURT OF INQUIRY

U. S. S. "IOWA" (first-rate),
KEY WEST, FLORIDA,
Monday, March 21, 1898, 10 A. M.

THE court met pursuant to the adjournment of yesterday.

Present: All the members and the judge-advocate.

The record of last day's proceedings was read over and approved.

The court was then cleared for deliberation.

After full and mature consideration of all the testimony before it, the court finds as follows:

1. That the United States battle-ship *Maine* arrived in the harbor of Havana, Cuba, on the twenty-fifth day of January, 1898, and was taken to buoy No. 4[1] in from five and a half to six fathoms of water by the regular government pilot.

The United States consul-general at Havana had

---

[1] Known at Havana as No. 4, of the United States Hydrographic but numbered 5 on Chart No. 307 Office.

Appendix C

notified the authorities at that place, the previous evening, of the intended arrival of the *Maine*.

2. The state of discipline on board the *Maine* was excellent, and all orders and regulations in regard to the care and safety of the ship were strictly carried out.

All ammunition was stowed in accordance with prescribed instructions, and proper care was taken whenever ammunition was handled.

Nothing was stowed in any one of the magazines or shell-rooms which was not permitted to be stowed there.

The magazines and shell-rooms were always locked after having been opened, and after the destruction of the *Maine* the keys were found in their proper place in the captain's cabin, everything having been reported secure that evening at 8 P. M.

The temperatures of the magazines and shell-rooms were taken daily and reported. The only magazine which had an undue amount of heat was the after ten-inch magazine, and that did not explode at the time the *Maine* was destroyed.

The torpedo war-heads were all stowed in the after-part of the ship, under the ward-room, and neither caused nor participated in the destruction of the *Maine*.

The dry guncotton primers and detonators were stowed in the cabin aft, and remote from the scene of the explosion.

Waste was carefully looked after on board the *Maine* to obviate danger. Special orders in regard to this had been given by the commanding officer.

Varnishes, driers, alcohol, and other combustibles of

Full Findings of the Court of Inquiry

this nature were stowed on or above the main-deck, and could not have had anything to do with the destruction of the *Maine*.

The medical stores were stowed aft, under the wardroom, and remote from the scene of the explosion.

No dangerous stores of any kind were stowed below in any of the other store-rooms.

The coal-bunkers were inspected daily. Of those bunkers adjacent to the forward magazines and shell-rooms, four were empty, namely, B3, B4, B5, B6. A15 had been in use that day, and A16 was full of New River coal. This coal had been carefully inspected before receiving it on board. The bunker in which it was stowed was accessible on three sides at all times, and the fourth side at this time on account of bunkers B4 and B6 being empty. This bunker, A16, had been inspected that day by the engineer officer on duty.

The fire-alarms in the bunkers were in working order, and there had never been a case of spontaneous combustion of coal on board the *Maine*.

The two after-boilers of the ship were in use at the time of the disaster, but for auxiliary purposes only, with a comparatively low pressure of steam, and being tended by a reliable watch.

These boilers could not have caused the explosion of the ship. The four forward boilers have since been found by the divers, and are in a fair condition.

On the night of the destruction of the *Maine* everything had been reported secure for the night at 8 P. M. by reliable persons, through the proper authorities, to

Appendix C

the commanding officer. At the time the *Maine* was destroyed the ship was quiet, and, therefore, least liable to accident caused by movements from those on board.

3. The destruction of the *Maine* occurred at 9:40 P.M. on the fifteenth day of February, 1898, in the harbor of Havana, Cuba, she being at the time moored to the same buoy to which she had been taken upon her arrival. There were two explosions of a distinctly different character, with a very short but distinct interval between them, and the forward part of the ship was lifted to a marked degree at the time of the first explosion. The first explosion was more in the nature of a report like that of a gun, while the second explosion was more open, prolonged, and of greater volume. This second explosion was, in the opinion of the court, caused by the partial explosion of two or more of the forward magazines of the *Maine*.

4. The evidence bearing upon this, being principally obtained from divers, did not enable the court to form a definite conclusion as to the condition of the wreck, although it was established that the after-part of the ship was practically intact, and sank in that condition a very few minutes after the destruction of the forward part.

The following facts in regard to the forward part of the ship are, however, established by the testimony:

A portion of the port side of the protective deck, which extends from about Frame 30 to about Frame 41, was blown up, aft, and over to port. The main-deck,

Full Findings of the Court of Inquiry

from about Frame 30 to about Frame 41, was blown up, aft, and slightly over to starboard, folding the forward part of the middle superstructure over and on top of the after-part.

This was, in the opinion of the court, caused by the partial explosion of two or more of the forward magazines of the *Maine*.

5. At Frame 17 the outer shell of the ship, from a point eleven and a half feet from the middle line of the ship and six feet above the keel when in its normal position, has been forced up so as to be now about four feet above the surface of the water, therefore about thirty-four feet above where it would be had the ship sunk uninjured.

The outside bottom plating is bent into a reversed V shape ($\wedge$), the after-wing of which, about fifteen feet broad and thirty-two feet in length (from Frame 17 to Frame 25), is doubled back upon itself against the continuation of the same plating, extending forward.

At Frame 18 the vertical keel is broken in two and the flat keel bent into an angle similar to the angle formed by the outside bottom plating. This break is now about six feet below the surface of the water, and about thirty feet above its normal position.

In the opinion of the court, this effect could have been produced only by the explosion of a mine situated under the bottom of the ship at about Frame 18 and somewhat on the port side of the ship.

6. The court finds that the loss of the *Maine* on the occasion named was not in any respect due to fault or

Appendix C

negligence on the part of any of the officers or members of the crew of said vessel.

7. In the opinion of the court, the *Maine* was destroyed by the explosion of a submarine mine, which caused the partial explosion of two or more of the forward magazines.

8. The court has been unable to obtain evidence fixing the responsibility for the destruction of the *Maine* upon any person or persons.

W. T. SAMPSON,
Captain U. S. N., President.

A. MARIX,
Lieutenant-Commander U. S. N.,
Judge-Advocate.

APPENDIX D

MESSAGE OF THE PRESIDENT OF THE UNITED STATES

To the Congress of the United States:

For some time prior to the visit of the *Maine* to Havana harbor, our consular representatives pointed out the advantages to flow from the visit of national ships to the Cuban waters, in accustoming the people to the presence of our flag as the symbol of good will and of our ships in the fulfilment of the mission of protection to American interests, even though no immediate need therefor might exist.

Accordingly, on the 24th of January last, after conference with the Spanish minister, in which the renewal of visits of our war-vessels to Spanish waters was discussed and accepted, the peninsular authorities at Madrid and Havana were advised of the purpose of this government to resume friendly naval visits at Cuban ports, and that in that view the *Maine* would forthwith call at the port of Havana.

This announcement was received by the Spanish government with appreciation of the friendly character of the visit of the *Maine*, and with notification of inten-

Appendix D

tion to return the courtesy by sending Spanish ships to the principal ports of the United States. Meanwhile the *Maine* entered the port of Havana on the 25th of January, her arrival being marked with no special incident besides the exchange of customary salutes and ceremonial visits.

The *Maine* continued in the harbor of Havana during the three weeks following her arrival. No appreciable excitement attended her stay; on the contrary, a feeling of relief and confidence followed the resumption of the long-interrupted friendly intercourse. So noticeable was this immediate effect of her visit that the consul-general strongly urged that the presence of our ships in Cuban waters should be kept up by retaining the *Maine* at Havana, or, in the event of her recall, by sending another vessel there to take her place.

At forty minutes past nine in the evening of the 15th of February the *Maine* was destroyed by an explosion, by which the entire forward part of the ship was utterly wrecked. In this catastrophe two officers and two hundred and sixty-four of her crew perished, those who were not killed outright by her explosion being penned between decks by the tangle of wreckage and drowned by the immediate sinking of the hull.

Prompt assistance was rendered by the neighboring vessels anchored in the harbor, aid being especially given by the boats of the Spanish cruiser *Alfonso XII* and the Ward line steamer *City of Washington*, which lay not far distant. The wounded were generously cared for by the authorities of Havana, the hospitals

Message of the President

being freely opened to them, while the earliest recovered bodies of the dead were interred by the municipality in a public cemetery in the city. Tributes of grief and sympathy were offered from all official quarters of the island.

The appalling calamity fell upon the people of our country with crushing force, and for a brief time an intense excitement prevailed, which in a community less just and self-controlled than ours might have led to hasty acts of blind resentment. This spirit, however, soon gave way to the calmer processes of reason, and to the resolve to investigate the facts and await material proof before forming a judgment as to the cause, the responsibility, and, if the facts warranted, the remedy due. This course necessarily recommended itself from the outset to the Executive, for only in the light of a dispassionately ascertained certainty could it determine the nature and measure of its full duty in the matter.

The usual procedure was followed as in all cases of casualty or disaster to national vessels of any maritime state. A naval court of inquiry was at once organized, composed of officers well qualified by rank and practical experience to discharge the onerous duty imposed upon them. Aided by a strong force of wreckers and divers, the court proceeded to make a thorough investigation on the spot, employing every available means for the impartial and exact determination of the causes of the explosion. Its operations have been conducted with the utmost deliberation and judgment, and while independently pursued, no attainable source of infor-

Appendix D

mation was neglected, and the fullest opportunity was allowed for a simultaneous investigation by the Spanish authorities.

The finding of the court of inquiry was reached, after twenty-three days of continuous labor, on the 21st of March, instant, and, having been approved on the 22d by the commander-in-chief of the United States naval force on the North Atlantic Station, was transmitted to the Executive.

It is herewith laid before the Congress, together with the voluminous testimony taken before the court.

Its purport is, in brief, as follows:

When the *Maine* arrived at Havana she was conducted by the regular government pilot to buoy No. 4, to which she was moored in from five and a half to six fathoms of water.

The state of discipline on board, and the condition of her magazines, boilers, coal-bunkers, and storage compartments, are passed in review, with the conclusion that excellent order prevailed, and that no indication of any cause for an internal explosion existed in any quarter.

At eight o'clock in the evening of February 15 everything had been reported secure, and all was quiet.

At forty minutes past nine o'clock the vessel was suddenly destroyed.

There were two distinct explosions, with a brief interval between them.

The first lifted the forward part of the ship very perceptibly; the second, which was more open, prolonged,

Message of the President

and of greater volume, is attributed by the court to the partial explosion of two or more of the forward magazines.

The evidence of the divers establishes that the after-part of the ship was practically intact and sank in that condition a very few moments after the explosion. The forward part was completely demolished.

Upon the evidence of a concurrent external cause the finding of the court is as follows:

At Frame 17 the outer shell of the ship, from a point eleven and a half feet from the middle line of the ship and six feet above the keel when in its normal position, has been forced up so as to be now about four feet above the surface of the water, therefore about thirty-four feet above where it would be had the ship sunk uninjured.

The outside bottom plating is bent into a reversed V shape (∧), the after-wing of which, about fifteen feet broad and thirty-two feet in length (from Frame 17 to Frame 25), is doubled back upon itself against the continuation of the same plating, extending forward.

At Frame 18 the vertical keel is broken in two and the flat keel bent into an angle similar to the angle formed by the outside bottom plating. This break is now about six feet below the surface of the water, and about thirty feet above its normal position.

In the opinion of the court, this effect could have been produced only by the explosion of a mine situated under the bottom of the ship at about Frame 18, and somewhat on the port side of the ship.

The conclusions of the court are:

That the loss of the *Maine* was not in any respect due to fault or negligence on the part of any of the officers or members of her crew;

Appendix D

That the ship was destroyed by the explosion of a submarine mine, which caused the partial explosion of two or more of her forward magazines; and

That no evidence has been obtainable fixing the responsibility for the destruction of the *Maine* upon any person or persons.

I have directed that the finding of the court of inquiry and the views of this government thereon be communicated to the government of her Majesty the Queen Regent, and I do not permit myself to doubt that the sense of justice of the Spanish nation will dictate a course of action suggested by honor and the friendly relations of the two governments.

It will be the duty of the Executive to advise the Congress of the result, and in the meantime deliberate consideration is invoked.

WILLIAM MCKINLEY.

EXECUTIVE MANSION, March 28, 1898.

APPENDIX E

ENSIGN POWELSON'S PERSONAL REPORT TO CAPTAIN SIGSBEE ON THE CAUSE OF THE EXPLOSION OF THE "MAINE"

U. S. S. "FERN,"
HAVANA, CUBA, March 20, 1898.

I BELIEVE the *Maine* was blown up by forces external to the ship. There is, to my mind, abundant positive proof of the fact, for we know accurately the condition of a large portion of the forward body of the ship.

First, consider the present condition of the ship, and see how far it bears out the hypothesis of an initial explosion in one of the forward magazines. The initial explosion, if it was internal, must have occurred in one of four places: the forward six-inch magazine between Frames 18 and 21; the six-pounder magazine between Frames 21 and 24; the reserve six-inch magazine on the port side between Frames 24 and 30; or the ten-inch magazine on the starboard side between the same frames.

Consider that an explosion occurred initially in the forward six-inch magazine, and see how far the condition of the ship in that vicinity supports the hypothesis.

Appendix E

Many six-inch powder-tanks have been found, and two of these have been found full of powder. One of these full tanks presents an appearance which was unquestionably produced by an approximately uniform pressure external to the tank. The metal of the tank has been pressed closely about the powder in such a manner that the metal was molded to the form of the powder, and shows longitudinally the angles formed by the prismatic grains as they were arranged in the bag.

This pressure to which I have referred was not sufficient to break the tank, and the temperature was not sufficient to ignite the powder. Almost every one of the battered and broken six-inch tanks presented the same longitudinal convolutions as were noticed in the full six-inch tanks.

A great many of the tanks contained unburned excelsior packing, and some still contained the bags in which the powder was put up. Many six-inch shells were found over the powder-tanks in the ten-inch magazine, and a few were sent up [by divers]. One of these shell had its wooden nose-block and its sling entirely intact.

There was absolutely no sign of burning anywhere about it. Many of these six-inch shell had the slings still attached.

Just forward of the six-inch magazine and next the ship's side on the port side was a store-room in which some old ropes and general stores were stowed. This room was fitted with horizontal boarding next the ship's side. A part of this store-room is now visible about

Ensign Powelson's Personal Report

two feet under water, and the boarding is still attached to the ship's side and is absolutely unburned. The side was bent at this store-room at about Frame 15 in such a manner that the outside plating aft of Frame 15 was folded against the side plating forward of Frame 15, which forms the side of the store-room, the outer or green sides of the plating being now adjacent. The angle of this fold was originally vertical, and followed Frame 15. The boarding is still attached to the plating of the forward half of the store-room, and projects aft intact beyond the fold at Frame 15.

If this folding of the side plating had been produced by a pressure from within the ship at about Frame 18, where the six-inch magazine was located, the boarding would have been pushed out with the side and would have been broken at Frame 15, where the angle of the fold occurs. Only a pressure from without, pushing the plating in forward of Frame 15, or an internal pressure applied some distance aft of Frame 15, could have produced the present condition of boarding and plating. If the six-inch magazine with its forward bulkhead at Frame 18 had been the seat of an explosion initial or secondary, and had blown the side plating out aft of Frame 15, it would also have blown the boarding against the side out, too. As it was, the boarding, which is only lightly secured to the frames, was pulled away from the side aft of Frame 15 by a bending produced by forces without the ship.

A large number of equipments, such as haversacks, knapsacks, canteens, and rubber blankets, were stowed

Appendix E

outboard just aft of this magazine. They were found in good condition and absolutely unburned. The inner skin and outer skin under the six-inch magazine are closer together than they were originally, but there is no evidence that this has been produced by a pressure above the inner skin. In fact, the appearance of the broken dogs which held down the manhole plate would indicate a pressure from underneath. All these details taken together preclude any possibility of an initial explosion at the forward six-inch magazine.

Consider the initial explosion as having occurred in the six-pounder magazine.

The inner skin under it is still attached to the frame, and shows no signs of having been blown down. The equipments—haversacks, etc., to which I have referred—were stowed outboard next this magazine, and were found intact. Many six-pounder shells have been found, but in none of them was the base fuse blown out, nor was the point at the nose broken, nor was an exploded shell found.

The shell in most cases have been detached from the brass case, and these cases have been found badly battered, some of them apparently having been exploded. Such explosion could not have occurred while the shell were still attached to the cases, or broken shell would have been found. Some six-pounder shell were sent up unexploded, with brass cases, though badly battered, still attached to them, and full of powder. These shell and cases were found over the shells and tanks of the ten-inch magazine. Had this six-pounder magazine been

Ensign Powelson's Personal Report

the point of initial explosion caused by fire within the ship, the additional heat and pressure produced by an explosion of the first few charges would have been sufficient, in all probability, to have fired most of the other charges.

Consider an initial explosion in the ten-inch magazine.

In this case the superstructure would not have been blown upward and from port to starboard, as is now the case. The main- and berth-decks would not have been raised on the port side as they are now in such a manner that the ship in the vicinity of the after-half of the superstructure has an apparent list to starboard, while that part of the ship aft of the superstructure has a decided list to port. The beam supporting the protective deck at the armor-tube is broken at the midship line, and the rivets on the starboard side are sheered sharply from port to starboard. The port side of the beam is bent sharply up against the conning-tower supports. The protective deck supporting the armor-tube and conning-tower supports is bent up on the port side and bent down on the starboard side of the armor-tube. All the shafting coming down through the armor-tube has been bent sharply from port to starboard where it comes through the protective deck. The fore-and-aft beam of the main-deck in the midship line just forward of the conning-tower supports has been broken where it crosses a thwartship beam, and both ends have been pushed sharply from port to starboard.

The light-box in the starboard ten-inch magazine bulkhead was found in very fair condition, and the

Appendix E

bulkhead was merely bent outboard and not blown through. There was still coal in the bunker on the outboard side of this bulkhead. On this bulkhead, which had been bent outward and down, and near the light-box, was found a manhole plate from the inner bottom. The tongue and groove boarding of the magazine, some of which was broken off by a diver and sent up, was found absolutely unburned. A ten-inch powder-tank was found full of powder. More were found in such good condition as to bar absolutely any possibility of having been exploded.

Many were found with the powder-bags still in them and with the excelsior packing unburned. Almost all the tanks had longitudinal convolutions such as I have referred to in the six-inch tanks. Many six-inch shell and many six-pounder shell are now lying on the powder-tanks of the ten-inch magazine, where they had evidently been thrown by the elevation of the keel to its present perpendicular form between Frames 18 and 23. The after-part of the ten-inch magazine is covered with debris to the height of ten or twelve feet. A great many ten-inch shell are still in the ten-inch-shell room, and some of them are still arranged symmetrically in their racks.

Where the ten-inch magazine bulkheads join the magazine floor the original right angle is approximately preserved, the bending of the magazine bulkheads being greatest at the upper part.

All these details and conditions disprove any theory of an initial explosion in the ten-inch magazine.

Ensign Powelson's Personal Report

Consider an initial explosion in the reserve six-inch magazine. Alongside of and just outboard of this magazine was a bunker full of coal containing forty-one and a half tons of coal. If the explosion of this magazine had been initial, caused by heat from without or spontaneous combustion from within, the pressure of gases in it would have increased until sufficient to burst the watertight bulkheads. If we consider that this was the case, and that on bursting the force of impact of the gases on the decks above was sufficient to lift the superstructure and conning-tower and double them back, then it must be admitted that an explosion of such force must certainly have blown out the two light coal-bunker bulkheads and the side plating, for their strength was little compared to that of the heavy decks above the magazine. Had these bulkheads and the side plating been blown out, coal would have been found in the mud on the port side in large quantities and for a considerable distance from the ship. But this was not found to be the case. Practically no coal or plating was found outboard of the line of the ship on the port side. The ten-inch shell were found in large numbers in the ten-inch-shell room, which was immediately adjacent to this magazine. The splinters of the wood backing still attached to the armor-plate aft of Frame 41 all pointed inboard, and the whole bottom of the ship forward of Frame 41 was lifted as a whole, although part of it in this vicinity was blown completely away and there is now no trace of it. The inner and outer skins of that part of the bottom still remaining have been pushed closer together, but the

Appendix E

inner skin has not been bulged downward between frames, and there is no evidence of an internal pressure having been applied to it. These details clearly show that while the reserve six-inch magazine, of which and of the contents of which we have no trace, may have been ignited by an external explosion under the ship on the port side, and may have aided in lifting and wrecking the superstructure, it could not possibly have been the seat of the initial explosion.

Consider now the condition of the forward body of the ship forward of Frame 43.

The keel is no longer in its original position. An accurate survey shows that the whole bottom of the ship has been lifted.

The keel rises at a gentle slope from Frame 43 to about Frame 22. It is then doubled back upon itself for a distance of about three feet through an angle of about 160°, and is then bent vertically upward, and the vertical keel is broken at Frame 18, and that part of the keel forward of Frame 18 has been turned to port through a horizontal angle of about 86° and bent downward through an angle of about 50°. The side plating has been pushed in, forming a V, the apex of which follows Frame 17 from the keel to a point five feet above the second longitudinal on the port side.

Another V has been formed by the side plating being bent in on the port side. The apex of this V follows Frame 15 from a point five feet above the second longitudinal to the water-line. The forward body of the ship forward of Frame 18 has been bent to port

Ensign Powelson's Personal Report

through a right angle nearly, and has been rolled over until it now rests in the mud on the starboard side.

The outer and inner bottom have been pushed together closer than originally throughout almost all that part of the ship between Frames 43 and 18, and the vertical keel and longitudinals are buckled to starboard.

The whole port side of the ship from Frame 26 to Frame 41 above the third longitudinal, about, is gone, and there is no definite trace of it. Aft of Frame 41 on the port side, for a distance of thirty feet, the side plating above armor has been blown in. The decks at this frame are inclined to starboard and aft, while the afterpart of the ship has a decided list to port. The splinters of the wood backing of the armor points inboard on the port side. The armor on the port side forward of Frame 41 is blown away. While the ship at Frame 41, by the position of her decks, appears to list to starboard, the bottom of the armor-plating of the port side is one foot in the mud, and a similar point on the starboard [side] is about twelve feet above the mud.

The starboard side of the ship, under water body, is blown outward forward of Frame 41, but is not blown away. The plating has been bent out, and now lies horizontal in the mud. Both coal and plating are found at a considerable distance from the starboard side in large quantities, while in similar places on the port side nothing but mud is found. The armor-plates on the starboard side forward of Frame 41 were blown out, leaving a part of their wood backing still attached to the plates aft of Frame 41, and projecting five feet farther

Appendix E

forward, with splinters all pointing outboard. The manhole plate, which was found lying on the starboard ten-inch magazine bulkhead near the light-box, had still attached to it half of the rim to which its hinges were attached and which secured it to the inner skin.

This plate had three small cracks on its under surface, and the rim was bent in such a manner as could only have been produced by a pressure from underneath lifting one end of the manhole plate, breaking the rim in two across the minor axis of the plate, and tearing the part of the rim now attached to the plate by one hinge from the inner skin. A rivet was still attached to this rim, and was bent into an arc, showing that the plate was lifted up at one end of its major axis, the other end acting as a center of motion. One of the cracks to which I have referred as having been produced by a pressure from below extended across the plate directly under and parallel to the heavy stiffener cast on the top side of the plate.

The second port longitudinal at Frame 17 is now above water. The strake of bottom plating containing a sea-valve between Frames 23 and 24 just above the second longitudinal is broken horizontally across the hole for the valve, and a radial crack runs down from the lowest point of the hole for a distance of about eight inches. This indicates a probable pressure from the outside of the ship, which, entering into the sea-valve, would act as a wedge, and would tend to crack and break the plate as has been done.

A hole six feet deep and fifteen feet in diameter was

Ensign Powelson's Personal Report

found in the mud, about a week after the explosion, forward where the keel at about Frame 6 now lies.

From the drawings showing the position of the keel in the vertical and horizontal planes, it is probable that before the explosion occurred the frames in the neighborhood of Frame 25 were over the point where this hole in the mud was found.

The ship was pushed violently from port to starboard and the moorings holding fast evidently bent the bow around to its present position. The whole present condition of the ship is incompatible with the theory of an initial inside explosion, and all known details and conditions bear out the hypothesis of a heavy external explosion on the port side. That part of the keel which was under the forward six-inch and six-pounder magazines is now vertical with the inner and outer skin, jammed together in places. The port side is blown in, and the starboard side is blown out. While the violence of the explosion was sufficient to blow away nearly sixty feet of the side from the second longitudinal to the main-deck, so that no recognizable trace remains, the force on the starboard side was merely sufficient to fold out the coal-bunker bulkheads and side plating to a horizontal position. The large horizontal angle made by the keel forward of Frame 18 and the keel aft of Frame 18 indicates a very heavy outside explosion on the port side. The side plating above armor on the port side at and for some twenty feet abaft the port crane was blown sharply in, while the armor under it, with its strong support, held fast. This is in a measure

Appendix E

an indication of the gradual decrease of the force of the explosion from its center, and indicates a heavy explosion of large area.

The finding of so many six-inch and six-pounder shell on top of the ten-inch powder-tanks indicates that these shell were spilled out of their magazines when the keel under them was elevated to its present vertical position, and that they are still on top of the ten-inch powder-tanks shows that there was no general explosion in the ten-inch magazine.

W. V. N. POWELSON,
Ensign U. S. N.

APPENDIX F

FINDING OF THE SPANISH COURT OF INSTRUCTION [INQUIRY]

To Admiral Manterola, Naval Commandant-General of the Station.

YOUR EXCELLENCY: On the night of February 15 last a dreadful and extraordinary event disturbed the usual tranquillity and internal order of this bay. A mournful catastrophe had occurred on board the North American ironclad *Maine*.

Having been instructed by your Excellency, in the letter which gave rise to the present proceedings, to proceed with all possible promptitude and energy to the investigation of the matter in question, I began my preliminary proceedings while the flames produced by the explosion were still rising from the vessel, and while some lesser [explosions,] caused, no doubt, by the action of the heat upon the shells and other explosives, were heard at intervals.

The undersigned immediately ordered all persons to be summoned who, owing to their being in the vicinity of the said vessel, could give any explanation or information with regard to the disaster, or any account

Appendix F

of its effects, and I requested the attendance of an official interpreter of the government, in order that he might act as such in the taking of such depositions as might necessitate his services, and I wrote to the consul of the United States of America in this capital, requesting the attendance of such of the principal officers and men of the crew of the *Maine* as might be in a condition to testify.

As Don Francisco Javier de Salas, a lieutenant in the navy, the secretary of the court of inquiry, was asked by an American officer, a few minutes before the beginning of the proceedings, whether the explosion could have been caused by a torpedo, notwithstanding the emphatic expressions of public opinion, which immediately rejected this supposition as absurd, and which were corroborated by arguments easily understood by every naval officer, I thought it expedient to direct the investigation along this line, on account of the facility of obtaining sufficient data to show the external action during the moments following submarine explosions, which are so peculiar in their character, and so well known to all who have witnessed them and studied them in their effects.

The North American man-of-war *Maine*, of 6682 tons displacement, made of steel, 318 feet in length, 57 feet beam, and 22 feet in depth, having double engines of 9293 indicated horse-power, launched in New York in 1890, entered this port on the 24th of January of this year, and anchored at buoy No. 4 (see the part of the plan at folio 101). The undersigned has heard unoffi-

Finding of the Spanish Court

cially the reason of the arrival and stay in these waters of the ironclad in question. For this it was sufficient to call to mind the royal order of August 11, 1882, which permits in ordinary times of peace the entrance of foreign squadrons and single vessels into our ports without any other restrictions than those prescribed by the ordinances of the navy, and that of obedience to the police regulations established in those ports.

Taking the said buoy No. 4 [locally No. 4, but No. 5 on Chart 307 of the United States Hydrographic Office] as the center, the depth of the bay varies, within a radius of a hundred meters, from thirty to thirty-six feet, with a bottom of loose mud. The *Maine*, when she came in, drew 22 feet, and the depth of the water at the place where she is sunk is 32 feet at the bow and 30 feet at the stern.

On the night of the sad occurrence the Spanish cruiser *Alfonso XII* was anchored at buoy No. 3, and the naval steam-transport *Legaspi* at No. 2, distant one hundred and forty and two hundred and forty meters, respectively, from the said buoy No. 4.

At the moment of the explosion there was no wind, and the water was very smooth, as it usually is in this bay at that hour.

The rise of the tide in the harbor is one and a half feet, and the high tide on that day was at 4 P. M.

Before proceeding to the consideration of other data, I think it well to recall to your Excellency's enlightened mind the phenomena which accompany the explosion of a submarine mine, meaning thereby what is

Appendix F

known under the generic term of torpedo, and leaving aside all that can apply exclusively to a subterranean mine, on account of the utter impossibility that such a mine could have been prepared without batteries [*elementos*], or even with batteries, without the knowledge of the authorities and of the public generally.

The ignition of the torpedo must necessarily have been produced either by collision or by electrical discharge; and as the state of the sea and the wind did not allow of any motion in the vessel, the hypothesis of a collision at that moment must be rejected, and we must consider that of an electric current sent by a cable [wire] from a station; but no traces or signs of any wire or station have been discovered.

The phenomena observed in submarine explosions are as follows: When the ignition takes place, the explosive substance is converted into a gaseous one and forms a bubble, which, owing to its ascensional force, tends usually to rise to the surface in a vertical line, producing a detonation more or less loud in proportion to the quantity of explosive material employed and the depth at which it is placed, and accompanied by a column of water, the height of which is likewise in proportion to the two circumstances mentioned.

At the same time a certain quaking [*trepidacion*] is noticed on the shore, which varies directly in proportion to the amount of explosive matter used, its greater immersion, and its nearness to the bottom; and, besides, a very peculiar shock is observed against the sides of vessels, which varies according to the distance, and

Finding of the Spanish Court

which, owing to the incompressibility of the water, does not, according to experiments, diminish in inverse proportion to the square of the distance.

Another important phenomenon, to which great weight should be attached in this case, on account of the peculiar nature of the harbor, is the presence of dead fish on the surface [of the water], usually caused by the rupture of the natatory bladder.

The action of torpedoes on vessels is very variable, and depends, besides, on the resistance of the hull which it strikes, the quantity of the explosive matter, and the distance.

No known case has yet been recorded where the explosion of a torpedo against the side of a vessel has caused the explosion of the magazines.

As is seen by the plans [diagrams], there was nothing but powder and shell in the forward magazines of the *Maine*.

It appears from the examination of witnesses:

Don Julio Peres y Perera, naval lieutenant of the first class, states in his deposition that he was in his sheers-house [*casa de la machina*], about four hundred yards from the said vessel, when, about 9:35 P. M., he saw an enormous blaze of fire rise toward the zenith and to a great height, followed by a terrible explosion. He adds that almost the whole of the ironclad was covered by a thick smoke, that the illumination was instantaneously extinguished, and that an infinite number of colored lights passed away into space. The moment after the explosion all was dark until, a little later, the awful scene was illuminated by the brightness of the fire, which was certainly caused by the explosion.

The witness says that other explosions, apparently of shell, followed, which continued until two o'clock in the morning, at which hour the fire began to diminish.

The witness saw the bow sink a few minutes after the explosion, and he asserts that there was no column of water, nor the least movement in the water [*mar*], and that there was no shaking of the land on the shore.

The other depositions of witnesses confirm the description of the explosion given by this officer, and they all agree that they noticed no movement in the water, and that they felt no shock of the water, although some of them were on board vessels as near the *Maine* as the *Alfonso XII*.

During the early hours of the morning the undersigned, accompanied by the secretary, made a close examination of the bay without finding any dead fish, or injuries of any kind on the piles of the piers.

Don Francisco Aldao, the head pilot, testifies (page 80 and back) that the harbor of Havana abounds in fish, and that there are persons who devote themselves to this industry with profit; and the technical assistant of the junta of the harbor works, Señor Ardois, who has been engaged upon them for many years, states that, without any exception, whenever small blasts have been made with charges [of powder] varying from five to twenty-five pounds, for the purpose of blowing up hulls of vessels, loose rock, and even shoals in the bay, a

Finding of the Spanish Court

great number of dead fish have been found inside the hulls or floating on the surface of the water.

For the purpose of procuring the greatest possible number of data, several experiments were made, to which the diagrams at pages 160 and 161 refer.

In continuation of the investigation, on the 16th of February the United States consul was requested, through your Excellency, to procure the attendance of some of the surviving officers and sailors of the *Maine*, in order to receive such testimony as they might see fit to give with regard to the occurrence. On the same day, through the same medium, permission was requested to examine the bottom of the vessel. On the 18th of February I again applied to your Excellency to procure from the commander of the *Maine*, either directly or through his consul, exact information as to the quantity of explosives still existing in that part of the vessel which had not been burned. On the 21st I went to the American steamer *Mangrove* for the purpose of having an interview with Mr. Sigsbee, the commander of the *Maine*, who expressed to me his wish that the Spanish investigators might be present at the operations of the American official diver. On the same day I again wrote, asking for permission to proceed to the examination of the ironclad. On the 22d I repeated my visit to the *Mangrove*.

On the 19th of February the authorities had replied, stating that, by agreement with the commander of the *Maine* and the United States consul-general, the examination requested in my letter of the 18th would be

Appendix F

made as soon as those gentlemen received the appliances and divers whom they had asked for.

On the 24th I received an important communication, dated February 17, inclosing one from his Excellency the governor-general of this island, stating that the commander of the *Maine,* upon being consulted as to the steps necessary to the success of this investigation, had replied that he expected to execute all the operations necessary to the examination of the vessel which had been under his command under his own supervision, in accordance with the provisions of the regulations of the American navy.

It was at last possible to make use of the new mode of investigation offered by the work of the divers, as it was discovered, from what they have accomplished up to this date, that the hull of the wrecked vessel is apparently buried in the mud, and that the examination of the outside is impracticable, but that it may be possible to examine the inside when the multitude of articles of all kinds which are lying in confusion in it have been removed.

The divers, having been instructed to examine and describe everything they might notice at the bottom of the bay and nearest to the sunken vessel, reported that they had not found in the mud which forms the bottom any inequalities or fissures—such as the examination of the bottom of the bay at the place occupied by the *Maine* and the hull [*calado*] of the vessel would doubtless have brought to light, on the supposition that a torpedo had been the cause of the catastrophe. This imaginary explosive apparatus [*artificio*] must necessarily, in this case, have been placed at the very bottom of the bay or very near it, and when it exploded would have caused the gases to react upon it, and, at the same time that it produced a greater effect upon the water upward, it would have made large fissures [*deformaciones*] in the mud.

It appears from the examination of the wreck of the *Maine*, part of which is afloat, made by the undersigned, the commandants of artillery, the commandant of engineers, and the commander of the torpedo brigade (the report of which appears at page 24), that, whatever may have been the original cause of the disaster, there is no doubt that there was an explosion in the forward magazine, which entirely destroyed the decks and bulkheads, which now display the appearance of a shapeless mass of boards, bars, and pipes of metal, very difficult to describe. In particular may be noticed a large fragment of the forward deck, which must have been raised in the most violent manner and bent double toward the stern by the forward stack-house, like an immense sheet of iron, with a considerable inclination to starboard, which, upon turning over, hurled out of the ship the forward turret, containing two guns, which was situated on the starboard side, and another gun with a shield, which was placed within the ship on the second deck. When the deck was bent double, as has been said, the smoke-stacks must have fallen. On the present upper side of this deck may be seen the beams and the knees which fastened them to the sides of the ship.

Appendix F

The whole stern is submerged, with the mainmast in place and intact, so much of it as can be seen above the surface of the water, including the lights [glasses] of the skylights of the cabin hatchways, and the glasses of one projector [*provector*].

The gentlemen above mentioned assert that the injuries described could only have been caused by the explosion of the forward magazine.

In order to give a better idea of the general appearance presented by that part of the ship which has been described, photographs were taken, which are shown on page 125 and following.

Notwithstanding what has been stated, it is proper to insist upon the fact that there is not a single instance on record, as has been already said, where the external action of the torpedo against the side of a vessel has caused the explosion of its magazines, although many vessels are recorded as having been totally destroyed by torpedoes, as may be proved by C. Sleeman's work entitled "Torpedoes and Torpedo Warfare," published in London in 1889, in which treatise there is a detailed account, extending from page 330 to page 338, inclusive, of the principal events of this nature which have occurred from 1585 to 1885; and this inventory of marine disasters includes a great number of United States men-of-war which destroyed Confederate vessels by means of torpedoes.

H. W. Wilson's treatise, Vol. II, published in 1896, and entitled, "Ironclads in Action; Naval Warfare from 1855 to 1895," may also be consulted on this subject.

Finding of the Spanish Court

On the other hand, there are recorded in the history of all the nations in the world, and especially in modern times, a proportionate number of events sufficing to prove the comparative facility with which ships of war are liable to become the victims of unknown and fatal accidents, owing to combinations which may result from the various and complicated materials employed in their construction and armament, as it is in many cases impossible to guard against them, except at the cost of terrible calamities.

The knowledge of the spontaneous combustion of the coal in the coal-bunkers is within the reach of all, and there is not a navy officer who cannot relate some sad episode attributed to this cause.

The danger is increased when the coal-bunkers are separated from the powder- and ammunition-magazines only by a bulkhead of iron or steel, and it becomes imminent when the heat developed in the coal is conveyed to the magazines, as has happened in several cases. To prevent them, recourse has been had to the study of a ventilation sufficient to prevent the accumulation of gases and the development of caloric, taking, in addition, the temperature of the coal-bunkers at proper intervals. In spite of all this, cases of spontaneous combustion have occurred repeatedly, and it is astonishing that the powder- and shell-magazines should still continue to be placed in immediate contact with the coal-bunkers.

Don Saturnino Montojo, an illustrious lieutenant in our navy, relates a very remarkable case which hap-

Appendix F

pened to the unfortunate *Reina Regente* when she was being built at Clydebank. Señor Montojo says that the shafts of the screws passed through several watertight compartments, which together formed a tunnel for the passage of the shaft. The compartment on the port side of that of the wheel of the helm was furnished with a register [*registro*] for the purpose of inspecting the shaft, and upon a workman attempting to draw out a small screw there was an explosion, causing a small fracture of the side on the exterior, and filling the stern compartments of the vessel with water; but the ship did not sink entirely, thanks to the other water-tight compartments and to the powerful pumps with which the ship was provided, which were set to work and kept her afloat.

This accident was attributed to the fact that the compartment in question had no ventilation. It is evident that gases are formed in any one of the places mentioned by the electric action developed by the fatty substances combined with the paint, the water, etc.

If there is any ventilation, these gases have an outlet; but if there is none, they accumulate and finally acquire a certain tension, and when they are brought into contact with a light or sufficient heat their explosion follows, as frequently occurs in mines and coal-bunkers. The eighty or ninety [coal-bunkers] of the *Reina Regente* had each a ventilation-pipe and a temperature-pipe. If, notwithstanding all this, any accident should obstruct or clog the ventilation, or if due attention is not paid to the temperature, or even when such attention is paid, if its indications are not good, the adoption of urgent measures of safety will merely diminish the danger, without making it disappear entirely.

The loss of the English vessel, the *Dotterel*, which has been so much studied and discussed, was due to the use of a drier [drying oil] employed in painting, and known under the name of the " zerotina drier."

In trade some of the varnishes and ingredients used in the painting of vessels are now recommended by protecting them with patents as not liable to produce inflammable gases.

The English scientific magazine, the " Engineer," No. 2189, of December 10, 1897, publishes an important article entitled " Shell Accident at Bull Point," showing the possibility of the explosion of a shell, not by the fuse, but by the spontaneous breaking of the shell itself. The shell of which the author of the article speaks was made for a four-inch gun, weighed twenty-five pounds, used the Leadenham fuse, and had a hardened point, tempered in water.

These instances suffice to prove that, in spite of all the precautions that may be taken, there may occur on board of modern vessels, especially war-vessels, many unforeseen accidents, arising from the combination of such diverse substances as those which are employed in their armament, so difficult and dangerous to manage, accumulated in large quantities and exposed to the action of heat and electricity almost constantly, each unhappy accident serving to regulate services on the basis of precautions, and to cause precautions to be

Appendix F

taken, so far as possible, with every new agent which necessity compels us to accept in the most recent constructions.

Consequently, in view of the result of the proceedings and the merits of the observations submitted, the undersigned considers it his imperative duty to state the following conclusions:

1. That on the night of February 15 last an explosion of the first order, in the forward magazine of the American ironclad *Maine*, caused the destruction of that part of the ship, and its total submersion in the same place in this bay at which it was anchored.

2. That it is learned, from the diagrams of the vessel, that there were no other explosive substances or articles in that magazine—the only one which exploded—than powder and shells of various calibers.

3. That the same diagrams prove that said magazine was surrounded on the port side, the starboard side, and partly aft by coal-bunkers containing bituminous coal, and which were in compartments adjoining the said magazine, and apparently separated from it only by metal bulkheads.

4. That the important facts connected with the explosion in its external appearances at every moment of its duration having been described by witnesses, and the absence of all the circumstances which necessarily accompany the explosion of a torpedo having been proved by these witnesses and experts, it can only be honestly asserted that the catastrophe was due to internal causes.

Finding of the Spanish Court

5. That the character of the proceedings undertaken, and respect for the law which establishes the principle of the absolute extraterritoriality of a foreign war-vessel, have prevented the determination, even by conjecture, of the said internal origin of the disaster, to which, also, the impossibility of establishing the necessary communication, either with the crew of the wrecked vessel, or with the officials of their government commissioned to investigate the causes of the said event, or with those subsequently intrusted with the issue, has contributed.

6. That the interior and exterior examination of the bottom of the *Maine* whenever it is possible, unless the bottom of the ship and that of the place in the bay where it is sunk are altered by the work which is being carried on for the total or partial recovery of the vessel, will prove the correctness of all that is said in this report; but this must not be understood to mean that the accuracy of these present conclusions requires such proof.

Believing that I have fulfilled all the requirements of Article 246, Title XIV, Chapter I, of the Law of Military Procedure of the Navy, in accordance with which, and with your Excellency's orders, this investigation has been made, I have the honor to transmit this report to your Excellency's hands, that you may come to a correct decision on the subject.

PEDRO DEL PEDRAL (Rubricated).

HAVANA, March 22, 1898.

APPENDIX G

NAMES AND RATES OF THE MEMBERS OF THE "MAINE'S" CREW AT THE TIME OF THE EXPLOSION, TOGETHER WITH THE ISSUE THEREFROM OF EACH MEMBER, AND THE NAME AND ADDRESS OF HIS NEXT OF KIN OR NEXT FRIEND, AS BORNE ON THE RECORDS OF THE NAVY DEPARTMENT

STATISTICAL SUMMARY OF KILLED, WOUNDED, SAVED, ETC.

Officers attached	26
Officers on board at explosion	22
Officers on shore at explosion	4
Crew attached	329
Crew on board at explosion	328
Crew at Key West at explosion	1
Total officers and crew attached	355
Total officers and crew at Havana	354
Total officers and crew on board at explosion	350
Officers killed	2
Officers on board saved	20
Officers on shore saved	4
Total officers saved	24

Appendix G

Crew killed at explosion	250
Crew died later of wounds at Havana	8
Total crew lost	258
Total officers and crew lost	260
Crew saved, wholly unhurt	16
Crew saved, injured (and lived)	54
Total crew saved (and lived)	70
Officers saved	24
Total officers and crew saved (and lived)	94

See pages 248–256 for the individual records.

Name	Rate	Issue from Explosion	Name and Address of Next of Kin
Adams, John T.	Coal-passer	Missing	Charles Adams, father, 1203 Half Street, S. W., Washington, D. C.
Aitken, James P.	Boatswain's Mate, 1st class	Missing	George Kessler, brother, Butte City, Mont. Allotment drawn by Louisa L. Aitken, Norfolk, Va.
Allen, James W.	Mess-attendant	Saved. Injured	Emma Allen, 435 Cumberland Street, Norfolk, Va.
Andersen, Holm A.	Coal-passer	Missing	Mrs. Petersen, mother, 4 Ocrequad, Christiania, Norway.
Anderson, Axel C.	Seaman	Missing	Lauritz Anderson, father, 3 Holgardansknein, F'd'ksburg, Copenhagen.
Anderson, Charles	Landsman	Missing	Anna Anderson, mother, 7 Lincoln Street, Norfolk, Va.
Anderson, Gustav A.	Seaman	Missing	Katerina Anderson, Uddevalla, Sweden.
Anderson, John	Boatswain's Mate, 2d class	Died. Identified	Julia Anderson, 541 First Avenue, New York, N. Y.
Anderson, John	Seaman	Missing	Andrew Anderson, father, Tonsberg, Norway.
Anderson, Oskar	Cockswain	Saved. Injured	Gustav Ericsson, father, Soderhamn, Sweden. Allotment drawn by Tina Anderson, New York, N. Y.
Andrews, Frank	Ordinary Seaman	Dead. Identified	Harry Andrews, father, Chemung, N. Y.
Anthony, William	Private	Saved. Uninjured	Albany, N. Y.
Auchenbach, Harry	Fireman, 2d class	Missing	Sarah Auchenbach, Newmanstown, Pa.
Aufindsen, Abraham	Cockswain	Missing	Marie Aufindsen, mother, Hornasandinas, Stavanger, Norway.
Augland, Bernhard	Blacksmith	Missing	Peter E. Augland, father, Ostersand, Sweden.
Awo, Firsanion	Steerage Cook	Saved. Injured	Ei Awo, mother, Mikawa, Japan.
Barry, John P.	Apprentice, 1st class	Dead. Identification positive	No relatives.
Barry, Lewis L.	Coal-passer	Missing	Annie Barry, mother, 91 Russell Street, Halifax, N. S.
Baum, Henry S.	Landsman	Missing	Emilie Baum, mother, 405 West 40th Street, New York, N. Y.
Becker, Jakob	Chief Machinist	Missing	Kate Becker, wife, 650 First Street, Hoboken, N. J.
Bell, John R.	Cabin Steward	Missing	No relatives.
Bennet, John	Private	Dead. Identification probable	286 East 26th Street, New York, N. Y.
Bergman, Charles	Boatswain's Mate, 1st class	Saved. Injured	John Hergman, father, Westerick, Sweden.
Blomberg, Fred	Landsman	Missing	August Blomberg, father, 65 Randolph Street, Chicago, Ill.
Bloomer, John H.	Landsman	Saved. Injured	Mrs. S. Tripp, mother, East Deering, Me.
Boll, Fritz	Bayman	Dead. Identified	Johanno Ecke, sister, 37 Murenstrum, Berlin, Germany.
Bonner, Leon	Seaman	Missing	Michael Bonner, 77 Washington Street, New York, N. Y.
Bookbinder, John	Apprentice, 2d class	Missing	Jacob Bookbinder, 343 North Second Street, Brooklyn, N. Y.
Botting, Vincent H.	Private	Missing	18 Mercer Street, New York, N. Y.
Boyle, James	Quartermaster, 1st class	Dead. Identification positive	Elizabeth Boyle, 546 West 53d Street, New York, N. Y.
Brinkman, Hennich	Seaman	Missing	Metta Kudenbusch, mother, Varel, Germany.
Brofeldt, Arthur	Chief Gunner's Mate	Missing	Laura Brofeldt, sister, Helsingfors, Finland.
Brosnan, George	Private	Missing	165 South Second Street, Brooklyn, N. Y.
Brown, James Thomas	Sergeant	Dead. Identification positive	Buncrana, Ireland.
Bruns, Adolph C.	Quartermaster, 3d class	Missing	Mrs. Augusta Bruns, mother, 206 West Conway Street, Baltimore, Md.
Bullock, Charles H.	Gunner's Mate, 2d class	Saved. Uninjured	John Bullock, father, 77 Ann Street, Newburg, N. Y.
Burkhardt, Robert	Quartermaster, 2d class	Dead. Identification probable	Louise Burkhardt, mother, 9 Louisendrape, Hambruck, Germany.
Burns, Edward	Coal-passer	Missing	James Burns, brother, 11 Jones Street, Charlestown, Mass.
Burns, James Robert	Corporal	Missing	162 43d Street, Brooklyn, N. Y.

Name	Rate	Issue from Explosion	Name and Address of Next of Kin
Butler, Frederick F.	Machinist, 2d class	Missing	Thomas Butler, father, 88 Central Avenue, Harrison, N. J.
Cahill, Francis D.	Landsman	Saved. Injured	Patrick Cahill, father, 12 Allen Street, Salem, Mass.
Caine, Thomas	Blacksmith	Missing	Bridget Caine, mother, 118 Henry St., Portsmouth, Va.
Cameron, Walter	Seaman	Missing	Ella Cameron, sister, Providence, R. I.
Carr, Herbert M.	Gunner's Mate, 2d class	Missing	William Carr, father, 1004 Second Street, Camden, N. J.
Caulfield, Wm. R. D.	Landsman	Missing	Mrs. M. M. Caulfield, mother, 2012 St. Peter's St., New Orleans, La.
Chingi, Suke	Mess-attendant	Missing	No relatives.
Christiansen, Carl A.	Fireman, 1st class	Missing	Martin Lassen, 128 De Graw Street, Brooklyn, N. Y.
Christiansen, Karrl	Fireman, 1st class	Saved. Injured	Butella Christiansen, mother, Stavanger, Norway.
Clark, Thomas	Coal-passer	Missing	Michael Clark, father, 13 Clover Street, Newark, N. J.
Clarke, James C.	Shipwright	Missing	James Clarke, father, 571 Eagle Avenue, New York, N. Y.
Cochrane, Michael	Fireman, 1st class	Missing	Michael Cochrane, father, 44 Central Street, Fall River, Mass.
Coffey, John	Private	Saved. Injured	13 Spring Street, Somerville, Mass.
Cole, Thomas M.	Bayman	Dead. Identification doubtful	Andrew J. Cole, 2734 Reese Street, Philadelphia, Pa.
Coleman, William	Ordinary Seaman	Missing	Emma Coleman, mother, 544 West 39th Street, New York, N. Y.
Coleman, William	Fireman, 2d class	Missing	Emma Coleman, mother, 272 Navy Street, Brooklyn, N. Y. Allotment drawn by Fannie Coleman, Brooklyn, N. Y.
Conroy, Anthony	Coal-passer	Dead.	Anthony Conroy, father, 5 K Street, Galway, Ireland.
Cosgrove, William	Fireman, 2d class	Dead.	No relatives.
Cronin, Daniel	Landsman	Saved. Injured	Mamie Cronin, sister, 298 Henry Street, New York, N. Y.
Curran, Charles	Cockswain	Dead. Identification positive	John Curran, father, Fort Hall, County Donegal, Ireland.
Dahlman, Berger	Seaman	Missing	Carl Dahlman, father, Oscarshamn, Sweden.
David, George	Ordinary Seaman	Saved. Injured	Emma David, mother, Madix, Malta.
Denrig, Charles	Seaman	Missing	Tilly Dennig, sister, Newark, N. J.
Dierking, John Henry	Drummer	Dead. Identification almost perfect	425 Fifth Avenue, Brooklyn, N. Y.
Dolan, John	Seaman	Saved. Uninjured	Clara Dolan, 53 Main Street, Brookline, Mass.
Donoughy, William	Ordinary Seaman	Dead. Identification positive	James Donoughy, father, Londonderry, Ireland.
Downing, Michael John	Private	Missing	South Boston, Mass.
Dressler, Gustav J.	Apprentice, 1st class	Saved. Injured	Gustav J. C. Dressler, father, 658 East 152d Street, New York, N. Y.
Drury, James	Fireman, 1st class	Missing	John Drury, father, 106½ Douglass Street, Brooklyn, N. Y.
Durckin, Thomas J	Ordinary Seaman	Saved. Injured	Mary Durckin, sister, 12 Ord Street, Salem, Mass.
Edler, George	Seaman	Missing	No relatives.
Eiermann, Charles F. W.	Gunner's Mate, 1st class	Dead. Identification positive	Charles Eiermann, Eberbach, Germany.
Erikson, Andrew V	Seaman	Died in San Ambrosio Hospital, Feb. 18	John Erikson, father, Helsingborg, Sweden. Allotment drawn by George Liedecker, New York, N. Y.
Fitts, John P.	Seaman	Missing	John W. Fitts, father, 87 Front Avenue, Rochester, N. Y.
Evensen, Carl	Seaman	Missing	Barbara Evensen, mother, 205 North Fourth Street, Brooklyn, N. Y.
Fadde, Charles F. J.	Apprentice, 1st class	Missing	John H. Fadde, father, 226 Franklin Street, Steindorn, Königsberg, Germany.
Falk, Rudolph	Oiler	Missing	Frederica Falk, sister, Sieindorn, Königsberg, Germany. Allotment drawn by Annie G. Falk, New York, N. Y.

Name	Rate	Issue from Explosion	Name and Address of Next of Kin
Faubel, George D.	Chief Machinist	Missing	George Faubel, father, 67 Jamaica Avenue, Baltimore, Md.
Fewer, William J.	Boatswain's Mate, 2d class	Dead. Identification probable.	Hannah Lash, sister, Providence, R. I.
Finch, Trubie	Apprentice, 1st class	Dead. Identification positive.	Henry Finch, father, Raleigh, N. C.
Fisher, Alfred J.	Oiler	Missing	Barnes Fisher, Newport, England. Allotment drawn by Thomas Fisher, Philadelphia, Pa.
Fisher, Frank	Ordinary Seaman	Died on board Spanish transport *Colon*, Feb. 20.	
Flaherty, Michael	Fireman, 1st class	Missing	Albert Barron, 890 Clum Street, Detroit, Mich.
Fleishman, Lewis M.	Seaman	Missing	Mrs. Michael Flaherty, wife, 300 First Street, Portsmouth, Va.
Flynn, Michael	Seaman	Saved. Injured	Rose Smith, aunt, 125 South Broadway, Baltimore, Md.
Flynn, Patrick	Fireman, 2d class	Dead. Identification probable.	Maggie Flanagan, aunt, 913 Hanover Street, Philadelphia, Pa.
Foley, Patrick J.	Apprentice, 1st class	Saved. Injured	James Flynn, Waterford County, Ireland.
Fougere, John	Coal-passer	Missing	Julia Leary, 16 Mechanic Street, Orange, N. J.
Fountain, Bartley	Boatswain's Mate, 1st class	Missing	Justick Fougere, mother, Arichat, Cape Breton.
Fox, George	Landsman	Saved. Injured	No relatives. Born in Quebec, Canada, Dec. 25, 1830.
Francke, Charles	Apprentice, 1st class	Missing	J. Franke, 459 Atlantic Avenue, Brooklyn, N. Y.
Furlong, James F.	Coal-passer	Missing	Lizzie Furlong, sister, South Cleveland, Ohio.
Gaffney, Patrick	Fireman, 1st class	Dead. Identification very probable.	Thomas Gaffney, Armaghcloughan, Keadue, County Roscommon, Ireland.
Galpin, C. P.	Private	Saved. Uninjured	Falls Church, Va.
Gardner, Frank	Coal-passer	Missing	No relatives. Allotment drawn by Helen Gardner, 164 East 78th Street, New York, N. Y.
Gardner, Thomas J.	Chief Yeoman	Missing	Edward Gardner, father, 480 Marcy Avenue, Brooklyn, N. Y.
Garrell, William M.	Fireman, 1st class	Saved. Uninjured	George M. Garrell, 696 Fourth Street, N. E., Washington, D. C.
Germond, Chester V.	Private	Saved. Injured	Poughkeepsie, N. Y.
Gordon, Joseph F.	Fireman, 1st class	Dead. Identified	Samuel Gordon, father, 825 County Street, Portsmouth, Va.
Gorman, William H.	Ordinary Seaman	Missing	Mary Gorman, mother, 3185 Washington Street, Boston, Mass.
Grady, Patrick	Coal-passer	Missing	William Grady, father, County Kildare, Ireland.
Graham, Edward P.	Coal-passer	Missing	Kate Markey, sister, 309 Seventh Street, Jersey City, N. J.
Graham, James A.	Chief Yeoman	Dead. Identification positive	Mrs. Emma Graham, wife, 62 Broadway, Newport, R. I.
Greer, William A.	Apprentice, 1st class	Missing	William Greer, 369 Manhattan Avenue, Greenpoint, Brooklyn, N. Y.
Griffin, Michael	Fireman, 2d class	Missing	Michael Griffin, 26 King Street, Dublin, Ireland.
Gross, Henry	Landsman	Dead. Identification positive	Louisa Gross, mother, 403 East 116th Street, New York, N. Y.
Grupp, Reinhardt	Coal-passer	Missing	Louisa Grupp, mother, 21 Cleveland Avenue, Chicago, Ill.
Hallberg, Alfred	Cockswain	Saved. Injured very slightly	Abraham Hallberg, father, Oroust, Iceland, Henan P. O., Sweden.
Hallberg, John A.	Oiler	Missing	Born in Guttenberg, Sweden, Jan. 13, 1861.
Ham, Ambrose	Apprentice, 1st class	Saved. Slightly injured	No relatives. Born in Guttenberg, Sweden, Jan. 13, 1861.
Hamburger, William	Landsman	Missing	Cephas Ham, 28 Catherine Street, Schenectady, N. Y.
Hamilton, Charles A.	Apprentice, 1st class	Missing	Frances Hamberger, sister, 35 Coles Street, Jersey City, N. J.
Hamilton, John	Chief Carpenter's Mate.	Missing	Samuel S. Hamilton, 90 11th Street, Newport, R. I.
Hanrahan, William C.	Cockswain	Missing	Margaret Hamilton, sister, 598 Nelson Street, Brooklyn, N. Y.
			John Hanrahan, Cohoes, N. Y.

Name	Rate	Issue from Explosion	Name and Address of Next of Kin
Harley, Daniel O'Connel	Fireman, 2d class	Missing	John Harley, 2116 Annin Street, Philadelphia, Pa.
Harris, Edward	Water-tender	Missing	M. Harris, sister, Binghamton, N. Y.
Harris, Millard F.	Quartermaster, 3d class	Dead. Identification probable	Millard Harris, father, Booth Bay Harbor, Maine.
Harris, Westmore	Mess-attendant	Saved. Uninjured	Westmore Harris, father, Charles City, Va.
Harty, Thomas J.	Coal-passer	Dead. Identification positive	Michael Harty, brother, 10 22d Street, New York, N. Y.
Hassell, Charles	Gunner's Mate, 3d class	Dead. Identification positive	Peter Hassel, father, Saba, W. I.
Hauck, Charles	Landsman	Missing	Wendell Hauck, father, 238 Graham Avenue, Brooklyn, N. Y.
Hawkins, Howard B.	Ordinary Seaman	Missing	Mary A. Hawkins, mother, West Bay City, Mich.
Heffron, John	Ordinary Seaman	Saved. Injured	Annie Heffron, wife, 1515 Dean Street, Brooklyn, N. Y.
Hennekes, Albert B.	Gunner's Mate, 2d class	Dead. Identification positive	John A. Hennekes, 420 Milton Street, Cincinnati, Ohio.
Herbert, John	Landsman	Saved. Injured	Hannah O'Brien, aunt, 548 Columbia Street, Brooklyn, N. Y.
Hermess, Alfred B.	Gunner's Mate, 3d class	Saved. Injured	No relatives. Born Trondhjeim, Norway, June 6, 1865.
Herriman, Benjamin H.	Apprentice, 1st class	Missing	Melvin H. Herriman, father, Chaptico, Md.
Holland, Alfred J.	Cockswain	Died in San Ambrosio Hospital, Feb. 19.	Patrick Holland, father, 60 15th Street, South Brooklyn, N. Y.
Holm, Gustav	Boatswain's Mate, 2d class	Dead. Identification very probable	Pauline Holm, mother, Horton, Norway.
Holzer, Frederick C.	Ordinary Seaman	Died in San Ambrosio Hospital, Feb. 25.	Andrew Holzer, father, 40 Union Avenue, Brooklyn, N. Y.
Horn, William J.	Fireman, 1st class	Dead. Identification probable	Annie Hart, sister, Whitehall, N. Y.
Hough, William L.	Landsman	Missing	Joseph Hough, brother, Madison Street, New York, N. Y.
Hughes, Patrick	Fireman, 1st class	Dead. Identification positive	James Hughes, father, Gengerborough, County Kings, Ireland.
Hutchings, Robert	Landsman	Saved. Injured	Zechariah Hutchings, father, 546 West 39th Street, New York, N. Y.
Ishida, Otogira	Steerage Cook	Missing	No relatives. Born Yokohama, Japan.
Jectson, Harry	Seaman	Died in San Ambrosio Hospital, Feb. 20.	
Jencks, Carlton	Gunner's Mate, 3d class	Dead. Identification very probable	William Jectson, father, Los Angeles, Cal.
			William Jencks, father, Farm Ridge, La Salle County, Ill.
Jernee, Fred	Coal-passer	Died in San Ambrosio Hospital, Feb. 19	William Jernee, father, 51 Water Street, New Brunswick, N. J. Allotment drawn by Abbie Jernee, York Street, Brooklyn, N. Y.
Johansen, Peter C.	Seaman	Missing	No relatives. Born Denmark, November 21, 1863.
Johnson, Alfred	Seaman	Saved. Injured	John Johnson, father, 14 Korsrand, Stockholm, Sweden.
Johnson, Charles	Ordinary Seaman	Missing	John Johnson, 11 Bond Street, Lynn, Mass.
Johnson, Charles Ehler	Private	Missing	
Johnson, George	Coal-passer	Dead. Identification probable	Elizabeth Johnson, mother, Washington.
Johnson, John W.	Landsman	Dead. Identification probable	Arthur Johnson, brother, United States Navy.
Johnson, Peter	Oiler	Missing	Jens Person, father, Silverberg, Sweden.
Jones, Thomas J.	Coal-passer	Dead. Identification positive	James Jones, brother, 316 La Salle Ave., Ottawa, Ill.
Jordan, William Joseph	Private	Missing	Tilton, N. H.
Just, Charles F.	Apprentice, 1st class	Dead. Identification positive	Mary A. Just, 7 Sires Street, Charleston, S. C.
Kane, Joseph H.	Landsman	Saved. Injured	No relatives. Born Worcester, Mass, October 29, 1868.

Name	Rate	Issue from Explosion	Name and Address of Next of Kin
Kane, Michael	Coal-passer	Missing	Honor Kane, mother, Camus Rosmuch P. O., County Galway, Ireland.
Kay, John A	Machinist, 1st class	Missing	Alexander Kay, father, Rising Star, Md.
Kean, Edward F	Private	Missing	Chicago, Ill.
Kelly, Frank	Private	Missing	262 D Street, South Boston, Mass.
Kelly, Hugh	Coal-passer	Missing	Thomas McPortland, uncle, 326 Sackett Street, Brooklyn, N. Y.
Kelly, John	Coal-passer	Missing	C. McShin, 79 Spencer Street, Brooklyn, N. Y.
Kesskull, Alexander	Seaman	Missing	Johan Kesskull, father, Kleinestrasse, Stettin, Germany.
Keys, Harry J	Ordinary Seaman	Dead. Identification almost perfect.	
Kihlstrom, Fritz	Ordinary Seaman	Missing	Henry Keys, Hartine, Washington.
Kinsella, Thomas F	Machinist, 2d class	Missing	Franz Kihlstrom, father, Gefle, Sweden.
			John Kinsella, father, 435 Harrison St., Anacostia, D. C., or Mrs. Thos. F. Kincella (claims to be wife), 318 11th St., S. E., Washington, D. C.
Kinsey, Frederick E	Machinist, 2d class	Missing	Emily Kinsey, mother, Stratford, Conn., or Mrs. Frederick E. Kinsey (claims to be wife), 77 Thomas Street, Newark, N. J.
Kitogata, Yukishi	Warrant Officer's Cook	Missing	Kiemon Kitogata, father, Kobé, Japan.
Kniese, Frederick H	Machinist, 1st class	Dead. Identification very probable	Frederick C. Kniese, Equitable Gas Light Co., Memphis, Tenn.
Koebler, George W	Apprentice, 1st class	Died in San Ambrosio Hospital, Feb. 22.	Maggie Sargent, 375 Douglass Street, Brooklyn, N. Y. Mrs. Margaret Koebler, 1317 Bushwick Avenue, Brooklyn, N. Y.
Kranyak, Charles	Apprentice, 1st class	Missing	No relatives. Born England, October 25, 1876.
Kruse, Hugo	Painter	Missing	William Kruse, father, Vine Street, Corona, Long Island, N. Y.
Kushida, Katsusaburo	Warrant Officer's Steward	Saved. Uninjured	Josko Kushida, father, 120 Otemashi, Hiroshima, Japan.
Laird, Charles	Master-at-arms, 3d class	Missing	Robert Laird, brother, 72 Linden Street, Everett, Mass.
Lambert, William	Fireman, 2d class	Missing	Susan Watts, sister, Wine Street, Hampton, Va.
Lanahan, Michael	Laudsman	Saved. Injured very slightly	John Lanahan, father, Louisville, Ky.
Lancaster, Luther	Boatswain's Mate, 2d class	Missing	No relatives. Born Feb. 16, 1872, at Fredericksburg, Va.
Lapierre, George	Apprentice, 1st class	Missing	Charles Lapierre, 1386 Rue St. Catherine, Montreal, Canada.
Larsen, Martin	Seaman	In hospital at Key West at time of explosion.	
Larsen, Peder	Seaman	Saved. Uninjured	Miss Hilda Larsen, Copenhagen, Denmark.
Lauriette, George M	Private	Missing	A. I. Engelsen, 170 Elizabeth Street, Brooklyn, N. Y.
Lawler, Edward	Coal-passer	Missing	Lowell, Mass.
League, James M	Chief Yeoman	Dead. Identification probable.	Mrs. Connolly, Liverpool, England.
Lee, William F	Apprentice, 1st class	Missing	John League, brother, 48 Conduit Street, Annapolis, Md.
Leene, Daniel	Coal-passer	Missing	Martha Steward, Ramsey, N. J.
Lees, Samuel	Ordinary Seaman	Dead. Identification positive	No relatives. Born Ansonia, Conn.
Leupold, Gustav	Fireman, 2d class	Missing	Samuel Lees, father, 7 West 116th Street, New York, N. Y.
Lewis, Daniel	Oiler	Missing	Juliane Leupold, mother, 310 Morris Avenue, Newark, N. J.
Lewis, John B	Water-tender	Missing	Charles Lewis, brother, 1014 19th Street, Washington, D. C.
Liebler, George	Apprentice, 1st class	Saved. Uninjured	Thomas Lewis, father, 17 Ann Street, Baltimore, Md.
Load, John H	Master-at-arms, 3d class	Saved. Injured	Mary Lieber, 510 East 18th Street, New York, N. Y.
Loftus, Paul	Private	Saved. Injured	No relatives. Scranton, Pa.
Lohman, Charles A	Coal-passer	Missing	G. Lohman, father, Upsala, Sweden.
Lorenzen, Jorgen J	Oiler	Missing	Anna Lorenzen, mother, Sanderberg, Germany.

Name	Rate	Issue from Explosion	Name and Address of Next of Kin
Losko, Peter Antonio	Private	Missing	132 North Fifth Street, Brooklyn, N. Y.
Louden, James W	Apprentice, 2d class	Dead. Identification doubtful	Annie Randolph, Keyport, N. J.
Lowell, Clarence E	Ordinary Seaman	Missing	Emery Lowell, father, South Gardiner, Maine.
Lund, William	Cockswain	Missing	C. Lund, mother, Bjormsborg, Finland.
Lutz, Joseph	Private	Saved. Uninjured	Passaic, N. J.
Lydon, John T	Ordinary Seaman	Missing	John Lydon, father, New York city.
Lynch, Bernard	Fireman, 1st class	Missing	Patrick Lynch, father, 418 Van Hrunt Street, Brooklyn, N. Y. Allotment drawn by Mary J. Leonard, Portland, Maine.
Lynch, Matthew	Coal-passer	Missing	Alexander Lynch, brother, Welden Street, Providence, R. I.
McCann, Harry	Seaman	Saved. Injured	Henry McCann, father, Sixth Street, Vallejo, Cal.
McGonigle, Hugh	Fireman, 2d class	Missing	Hugh McGonigle, father, County Donegal, Ireland.
Mack, Thomas	Landsman	Saved. Injured	William Mack, father, 71 West Lombard Street, Baltimore, Md
McDermott, John	Private	Missing	New York, N. Y.
McDevitt, William	Private	Saved. Injured	Listowel, Ireland.
McGuinness, William	Private	Saved. Injured	County Tyrone, Ireland.
McKay, Edward	Private	Saved. Uninjured	Hartford, Conn.
McManus, John J	Fireman, 2d class	Dead. Identification positive	James McManus, father, Ripley Street, Davenport, Iowa.
McNair, William	Ordinary Seaman	Saved. Injured	John McNair, father, 248 Emerson Street, Pitusburg, Pa.
McNiece, Francis J	Coal-passer	Dead. Identification very probable	Lucy McNiece, mother, 41 Warren Street, Charlestown, Mass.
Magaminc, Tomekichi	Mess-attendant	Missing	No relatives. Born May 24, 1871, Japan.
Malone, Michael	Fireman, 2d class	Missing	John Redden, 406 West 26th Street, New York, N. Y.
Marsden, Benjamin L	Apprentice, 1st class	Missing	John F. Marsden, father, Jersey City, N. J.
Marshall, John E	Landsman	Missing	William J. Marshall, brother, Cincinnati, Ohio; or V. C. Marshall, Henderson, Ky.
Martensson, Johan	Gunner's Mate, 3d class	Missing	Jens Martensson, brother, 22 Gamle Mont, Copenhagen, Denmark.
Mason, James H	Landsman	Missing	J. H. Fox (claims to be father), 233 Walworth Street, Brooklyn, N. Y.; or William Barnes, friend, 381 Fifth St., Jersey City, N. J.
Mattisen, Carl	Seaman	Missing	Henrietta Muller, 1701 Spruce Street, Philadelphia, Pa.
Mattsen, William	Ordinary Seaman	Saved. Injured	Peter Mattisen, 1109 South Fremont Street, West Bay City, Mich.
Matsen, Edward	Ordinary Seaman	Saved. Injured	Matsen Person, father, Skillinger, Sweden.
Matza, John	Coal-passer	Dead. Identification doubtful	Anna Matza, mother, 604 Illinois Avenue, East St. Louis, Ill.
Meehan, Michael	Sergeant	Saved. Uninjured	County Sligo, Ireland.
Meilstrup, Elmer M	Ordinary Seaman	Missing	J. S. Meilstrup, West Bay City, Mich.
Melville, Thomas	Coal-passer	Saved. Uninjured	No relatives. Born April 15, 1868, New York, N. Y.
Mero, Eldon H	Chief Machinist	Dead. Identification positive	Susan J. Mero, 2212 Cleveland Avenue, Philadelphia, Pa. Draws allotment.
Merz, John	Landsman	Missing	Francis M. Merz, father, 364 Bushwick Avenue, Brooklyn, N. Y.; or Elizabeth Merz, father, 143 Jefferson Street, Brooklyn, N. Y.
Mikkelsen, Peter	Seaman	Saved. Injured very slightly	Niels M. Mikkelsen, father, Overgaade, Abeltoft, Denmark.
Miller, George	Seaman	Missing	Mrs. Mary Howard, sister, 63 Pearl Street, New York, N. Y.
Miller, William S	Apprentice, 2d class	Missing	Ernest Petsch, father, 2152 Second Avenue, New York, N. Y.
Mobles, George	Cockswain	Missing	No relatives. Born March 11, 1866, Cephalonia, Greece.

Name	Rate	Issue from Explosion	Name and Address of Next of Kin
Monahan, Joseph Patrick	Private	Missing	156 Terrace Street, Roxbury, Mass.
Monfort, William	Landsman	Missing	Rollins, Monfort, Council Bluffs, Iowa.
Moore, Edward H	Coal-passer	Missing	Born Charles City, Va.
Morimere, Louis	Seaman	Saved. Injured	Louisa Merchant, 233 Normandy Street, Havre, France.
Moss, Gerhard C	Machinist, 1st class	Missing	Teresa Moss, wife, 788 27th Street, Brooklyn, N. Y. Draws allotment.
Moss, John H	Landsman	Missing	Jane Moss, Rainwood, N. C.
Mudd, Noble T	Seaman	Dead. Identification probable	Lewis Mudd, 302 G Street, S. E., Washington, D. C.
Murphy, Cornelius	Oiler	Missing	Bartholomew Murphy, Roberts Cove, County Cork, Ireland.
Newton, C. J	Private	Missing	632 East 136th Street, New York, N. Y.
Nielsen, John C	Fifer	Missing	Washington, D. C.
Nielsen, Sophus	Seaman	Missing	Marie Nielsen, mother, Fredericksund, Copenhagen, Denmark.
Noble, William	Cockswain	Dead	Peder Nielsen, father, 49 Overgordle, Odensee, Denmark.
	Fireman, 2d class	Missing. Identification probable	John Noble, father, Portland, Koskey, County Sligo, Ireland; or Mrs. Jane Powers, sister, East 27th Street, New York, N. Y.
Nolan, Charles M	Gunner's Mate, 3d class	Missing	John Nolan, brother, 126 Emerson Street, Boston, Mass.
O'Connor, James	Chief Boatswain's Mate	Missing	Phillip O'Connor, father, Bayonne City, N. J. Draws allotment.
O'Hagan, Thomas J	Apprentice, 1st class	Missing	No relatives. Born New York, N. Y.
Ohye, Mas	Mess-attendant	Missing	No relatives. Born Aug. 25, 1870, Japan.
O'Neill, Patrick	Fireman, 2d class	Missing	Margaret O'Neill, mother, Callenford, County Louth, Ireland.
Ording, Gustav C	Carpenter's Mate, 3d class	Missing	Elizabeth Sablehous, mother, Sixth and Patterson Streets, Newport, Ky.
O'Regan, Henry H	Water-tender	Missing	Catherine O'Regan, 413 Chelsea Street, East Boston, Mass. Draws allotment.
Paige, Frederick	Landsman	Missing	Nellie Smith, sister, 1884 Niagara Street, Buffalo, N. Y.
Palmgren, John	Seaman	Missing	John Palmgren, father, Allrun, Helsingborg, Sweden.
Panck, John H	Fireman, 1st class	Saved. Injured	Louis Panck, father, Lynchburg, Va.
Perry, Robert	Mess-attendant	Missing	Ida Perry, mother, 84 Nicholson Street, Norfolk, Va.
Phillips, Francis C	Apprentice, 1st class	Dead. Identification positive.	Ellery P. Phillips, father, 21 South Stewart Street, Rochester, N. Y.
Pilcher, Charles F	Ordinary Seaman	Saved. Injured	Robert Pilcher, uncle, 18 Webster Place, Detroit, Mich.
Pinkney, James	Mess-attendant	Dead. Identification doubtful	Mrs. Grace Pinkney, 8 South Street, Annapolis, Md. Allotment drawn by Eva F. Pinkney, Norfolk, Va.
Porter, John	Coal-passer	Missing	Jane Reyers, sister, Tom's Ridge, Westchester County, New York. Draws allotment.
Powers, John	Oiler	Missing	Margaret Powers, Crosshaven, County Cork, Ireland.
Price, Daniel	Fireman, 1st class	Dead. Identification probable.	Kate Price, mother, Stoneham, Mass.
Quigley, Thomas J	Plumber and Fitter	Missing	John Quigley, 862 10th Avenue, New York, N. Y. Draws allotment.
Quinn, Charles P	Oiler	Missing	Mary E. Miniard, 101 Fourth Street, Chelsea, Mass. Allotment drawn by Edward Joseph Miniard, Boston, Mass.
Rau, Arthur	Seaman	Saved. Injured	No relatives. Born Stettin, Germany, Dec. 10, 1873.
Redlen, Martin	Seaman	Saved. Uninjured	Adolph Reden, father, Mouestry Street, Union Hill, N. J.

Name	Rate	Issue from Explosion	Name and Address of Next of Kin
Reilly, Joseph	Fireman, 1st class	Missing	John Reilly, 246 Henry Street, New York, N. Y.
Richards, Walter E.	Apprentice, 2d class	Saved. Injured	Samuel N. Richards, Westville, N. J.
Richter, A. H.	Corporal	Missing	Chicago, Ill.
Rieger, William A.	Gunner's Mate, 1st class	Missing	Daisy Rieger, wife, Washington, D. C.
Rising, Newell	Coal-passer	Missing	Elihu Rising, father, Portchester, N. J.
Roberts, James Henry	Private	Dead. Identification very probable.	
Robinson, William	Landsman	Missing	Randolph, Mass. Lillian Laverty, sister, 1004 Garden Street, Hoboken, N. J. Allotment drawn by Mrs. Mary C. Stein, 808 Garden Street, Hoboken, N. J.
Roos, Peter	Sailmaker	Missing	Carlina Roos, Christianstad, Sweden.
Rowe, James	Ship's Cook, 4th class	Saved. Injured	No relatives. Born March 15, 1890, Tottenham, England.
Rusch, Frank	Ordinary Seaman	Saved. Injured	Joseph Rusch, father, Detroit, Mich.
Rushworth, William	Chief Machinist	Dead. Identification probable	Margaret Rushworth, wife, 202 Church Street, Norfolk, Va. Draws allotment.
Safford, Clarence F.	Gunner's Mate, 1st class	Missing	Charles Safford, High Street, Taunton, Mass.
Salmin, Michael E.	Ordinary Seaman	Missing	Eliza Salmin, sister, Libau, Russia.
Schoen, Joseph	Corporal	Dead. Identification doubtful	New York, N. Y.
Schroeder, August	Ordinary Seaman	Missing	John Schroeder, father, 24 Catherine Street, Brooklyn, N. Y.
Schwartz, George	Ship's Cook, 1st class	Saved. Injured	No relatives. Born Hanover, Germany, May 9, 1857.
Scott, Charles A.	Carpenter's Mate, 2d class	Dead. Identification doubtful	Andrew Scott, father, Freeport, Long Island.
Scully, Joseph	Boiler-maker	Dead. Identification very probable	James Scully, father, 1439 Henry Street, Baltimore, Md.
Seery, Joseph	Fireman, 1st class	Dead. Identification almost perfect.	Michael Seery, father, Naas, County Kildare, Ireland.
Sellers, Walter	Apothecary	Dead. Identification positive	John L. Sellers, Shelby, Ohio.
Shea, Jeremiah	Coal-passer	Saved. Injured	Cornelius Shea, father, 36 Winter Street, Haverhill, Mass.
Shea, John J.	Coal-passer	Missing	Ellen Shea, mother, 107 Mott Street, New York, N. Y.
Shea, Patrick J.	Fireman, 1st class	Missing	Michael Shea, father, Willimantic, Conn.
Shea, Thomas	Landsman	Missing	Dennis Shea, father, 148 East 36th Street, New York, N. Y.
Sheridan, Owen	Fireman, 2d class	Dead. Identification almost perfect.	
Shillington, John H.	Yeoman, 3d class	Missing	Joseph Sheridan, father, Arm, County Cavan, Ireland.
Simmons, Alfred	Coal-passer	Dead. Identification very probable	J. Shillington, 216 East Indiana Street, Chicago, Ill.
Smith, Carl A.	Seaman	Died in San Ambrosio Hospital, Feb. 18	Mrs. Emma Ruffin, mother, 105 Fayette Street, Portsmouth, Va.
Smith, Nicholas J.	Apprentice, 1st class	Dead. Identification probable	No relatives. Born June 15, 1874, at Hamburg, Germany.
Stevenson, Nicholas	Seaman	Missing	Mrs M. C. Smith, mother, Lynchburg, Va.
Stock, H. E.	Private	Missing	Severin Stevenson, father, Christiansand, Norway.
Strongman, James	Private	Missing	New York, N. Y. Prince Edward's Island.
Sugisaki, Isa	Ward-room Steward	Missing	Sabe Sugisaki, brother, Takata, Muro Odawara Kaoagawa, Japan.

Name	Rate	Issue from Explosion	Name and Address of Next of Kin
Suman, E. B.	Private	Dead	Hagerstown, Md.
Sutton, Frank	Fireman, 2d class	Dead	Identification doubtful. Born Galveston, Texas, March 10, 1868. No relatives.
Suzuki, Kashotaro	Mess-attendant	Dead	Identification positive. Born June 17, 1868, in Japan. No relatives.
Talbot, Frank C.	Landsman	Missing	Identification probable. William H. Talbot, father, Middle Street, Bath, Maine.
Teackle, Harry	Seaman	Saved. Injured	Annie P. Teackle, mother, 14 Stuyvesant Place, St. George, N. Y.
Tchan, Daniel J	Coal-passer	Missing	Jeremiah Tchan, father, 71 Division Street, New York, N. Y. Draws allotment.
Thompson, George	Landsman	Saved. Injured	No relatives. Born Aug. 6, 1854, Ionian Islands, Greece.
Thompson, T. G	Corporal	Saved. Injured	Charlestown, Mass.
Thompson, William H.	Landsman	Dead	Identification doubtful. Timothy O'Connor, 202 Elm Street, New York, N. Y.
Tigges, Frank B.	Coppersmith	Missing	Gerhard Brandkamp, 191 Ruge Street, Oelde, Germany.
Timpany, E. B	Private	Dead	Identification positive. Born in Digby, Nova Scotia.
Tinsman, William H	Landsman, 1st class	Saved. Injured	William H. H. Tinsman, father, East Deering, Maine.
Todoresco, Constantin	Fireman, 1st class	Missing	Maria A. Borche, Brala, Roumania.
Toppin, Daniel G.	Ward-room Cook	Saved. Injured	Elizabeth A. Toppin, wife, 304 West 39th Street, New York, N. Y.
Troy, Thomas	Coal-passer	Missing	No relatives. Born Jan. 7, 1869, Waterbury, Conn.
Tuohey, Martin	Coal-passer	Saved. Uninjured	Margaret Tuohey, mother, 372 Hicks Street, Brooklyn, N. Y.
Turpin, John H.	Mess-attendant	Missing	Dee Turpin, mother, Long Branch, N. Y.
Van Horn, H. A.	Private	Dead	Identification doubtful. Philadelphia, Pa.
Wagner, Henry	First Sergeant	...	Durkheim, Germany.
Wallace, John	Ordinary Seaman	Missing	Thomas Wallace, father, 43 I Street, South Boston, Mass.
Walsh, Joseph F	Cockswain	Missing	James H. Walsh, 25 Blaine Street, Brockton, Mass.
Warren, Asa V	Private	Missing	Craven County, N. C.
Warren, John	Fireman, 2d class	Missing	William Warren, father, Randolph, S. C.
Waters, Thomas J.	Landsman	Saved. Injured	No relatives. Born May 24, 1874, Philadelphia, Pa.
Webber, Martin V.	Landsman	Saved. Injured	Sarah Lawford, mother, Bar Harbor, Maine.
White, Charles O.	Chief Master-at-arms	Missing	Mrs. C. O. White, wife, 67 Poplar Street, Brooklyn, N. Y. Draws allotment.
White, John E.	Landsman	Saved. Injured	Luke White, father, 146 Nassau St., Brooklyn, N.Y. Draws allotment.
White, Robert	Mess-attendant	Dead	Identification probable. Caroline White, mother, King Street, Portsmouth, Va. Draws allotment.
Whiten, George	Seaman	Missing	Sarah Whiten, Middleburg, Va.
Wickstrom, John E.	Seaman	Missing	Henry Wickstrom, father, Helsingfors, Finland.
Wilbur, Benjamin R	Cockswain	Saved. Injured	Isaiah Wilbur, 1806 South Street, Philadelphia, Pa. Draws allotment.
Wilbur, George W.	Apprentice, 1st class	Missing	Isaiah Wilbur, 1806 South Street, Philadelphia, Pa.
Williams, Henry	Cabin Cook	Saved. Injured	Mrs. Henry Williams, 2 Hay Street, Richmond, Va.
Williams, James	Gunner's Mate, 3d class	Saved. Injured	Margaret Williams, wife, 25 West 18th Street, New York, N. Y.
Willis, A. O	Apprentice, 2d class	Saved. Injured very slightly	Catherine Willis, Keyport, N. J.
Wilson, Albert	Private	Missing	Philadelphia, Pa.
Wilson, Robert	Seaman	Missing	Anna M. Wilson, 17 Bond Street, Chicago, Ill.
Ziegler, John H	Chief Quartermaster	Missing	Mamie Wilson, New York. Draws allotment.
	Coal-passer	Missing	Jacob Ziegler, father, 124 Nelson Street, New Brunswick, N. J.

APPENDIX H

BURIAL AND IDENTIFICATION LIST OF THE REMAINS OF THE "MAINE'S" DEAD, FROM THE RECORDS OF CHAPLAIN J. P. CHIDWICK, U. S. N., TO MARCH 26, 1898, WITH ADDITIONS MADE THEREAFTER BY CAPTAIN C. D. SIGSBEE, U. S. N., FROM THE RECORDS OF THE NAVY DEPARTMENT

SUMMARY OF MORTUARY STATISTICS

Officers killed	2
Officers' bodies recovered and identified	1
Officers missing	1
Crew killed at explosion	250
Crew injured, and died later at Havana	8
Total crew lost	258
Dead of crew recovered and actually or supposedly identified	73
Dead of crew recovered but not identified	118
Total crew buried	191
Crew missing	67
Officer buried at Allegheny Cemetery, Pittsburg, Pennsylvania	1
Crew buried at Colon Cemetery, Havana	166
Crew buried at Key West	25

See pages 258–270 for the list.

Serial No.	Name	Rate	Character of Identification	Place of Burial	No. of Coffin	Row	Grave	Situation
1	Dierking, John H.	Drummer	Identification almost perfect	Colon Cemetery	1	1	1	Lowest right.
2	Graham, James A.	Chief Yeoman	Positive identification	Colon Cemetery	2	1	1	Lowest left.
3	Tinsman, William H.	Landsman	Positive identification	Colon Cemetery	3	1	1	Next to lowest right.
4	Brown, James T.	Sgt. Marines	Positive identification	Colon Cemetery	4	1	1	Next to lowest left.
5	Mero, Eldon H.	Ch. Machinist	Positive identification	Colon Cemetery	5	1	1	Top right.
6	Keys, Harry J.	Ord. Seaman	Identification almost perfect	Colon Cemetery	6	1	1	Top left.
7	....	....	Unrecognizable trunk of a boy	Colon Cemetery	7	1	2	Lowest right.
8	Sheridan, Owen	Fireman, 2d cl.	Identification almost perfect	Colon Cemetery	8	1	2	Lowest left.
9	....	....	Unrecognizable trunk of a boy	Colon Cemetery	9	1	2	Next to lowest right.
10	Gaffney, Patrick	Fireman, 1st cl.	Identification very probable.	Colon Cemetery	10	1	2	Next to lowest left.
11	Cosgrove, William	Fireman, 2d cl.	Positive identification	Colon Cemetery	11	1	2	Top right.
12	Seery, Joseph	Fireman, 1st cl.	Identification almost perfect	Colon Cemetery	12	1	2	Top left.
13	....	Fireman	Unrecognizable	Colon Cemetery	13	1	3	Lowest right.
14	....	....	Mass of flesh and bones	Colon Cemetery	14	1	3	Lowest left
15	....	....	Norwegian, very large and greatly swollen.	Colon Cemetery	15	1	3	Next to lowest right.
16	....	Fireman	Unrecognizable.	Colon Cemetery	16	1	3	Next to lowest left.
17	....	....	Only trunk and limbs	Colon Cemetery	17	1	3	Next to top right.
18	....	....	Body crushed, unrecognizable; only trunk and limbs	Colon Cemetery	18	1	3	Next to top left.
19	....	....	Body crushed, unrecognizable	Colon Cemetery	19	1	3	Top right.
20	....	....	Body crushed, unrecognizable	Colon Cemetery	20	1	3	Top left.
21	....	....	Body crushed, unrecognizable	Colon Cemetery	21	2	1	Lowest right.
22	Roberts, James H.	Private Marine	Identification very probable.	Colon Cemetery	22	2	1	Lowest left.
23	....	Fireman	Small in stature and with small features and red hair	Colon Cemetery	23	2	1	Next to lowest right
24	....	Coal-passer or Fireman	Small, stout, dark complexion, and about 35 years of age	Colon Cemetery	24	2	1	Next to lowest left.
25	....	....	Unknown, short and stout	Colon Cemetery	25	2	1	Top right.
26	Smith, Carl A.	Seaman	Died in the Hospital of San Ambrosio, Feb. 18	Colon Cemetery	26	2	1	Top left.
27	Erikson, Andrew V.	Seaman	Died in San Ambrosio Hospital, Feb. 18.	Colon Cemetery	27	2	2	Lowest right.
28	....	....	The following 24 bodies (Nos. 28 to 51) were brought to the cemetery during the grand civic funeral. I did not have an opportunity to see them, owing to a misunderstanding with the undertaker. They were placed in the 2d and	Colon Cemetery	28	2	2	
29	....	....		Colon Cemetery	29	2	2	
30	....	....		Colon Cemetery	30	2	2	
31	....	....		Colon Cemetery	31	2	2	
32	....	....		Colon Cemetery	32	2	2	
33	....	....		Colon Cemetery	33	2	3	
34	....	....		Colon Cemetery	34	2	3	

Serial No.	Name	Rate	Character of Identification	Place of Burial	No. of Coffin	Row	Grave	Situation
35			3d graves of the 2d row and in the 1st grave of the 3d row. In three instances the small remains of two bodies were placed in one coffin.	Colon Cemetery	35	2	3	
36				Colon Cemetery	36	2	3	
37				Colon Cemetery	37	2	3	
38				Colon Cemetery	38	2	3	
39				Colon Cemetery	39	2	3	
40				Colon Cemetery	40	2	3	
41				Colon Cemetery	41	2	3	
42				Colon Cemetery	42	3	3	
43				Colon Cemetery	43	3	1	
44			(Twenty-four bodies, Nos. 28 to 51)	Colon Cemetery	44	3	1	
45				Colon Cemetery	45	3	1	
46				Colon Cemetery	46	3	1	
47				Colon Cemetery	47	3	1	
48				Colon Cemetery	48	3	1	
49				Colon Cemetery	49	3	2	
50				Colon Cemetery	50	3	2	
51				Colon Cemetery	51	3	2	The situation in the grave of these eight bodies (Nos. 52 to 59) was not noted by the superintendent of the graves.
52	McManus, John J.	Fireman, 2d cl.	Positive identification	Colon Cemetery	52	3	2	
53		Fireman	Unrecognizable body	Colon Cemetery	53	3	2	
54			Unrecognizable body	Colon Cemetery	54	3	2	
55	Hassel, Charles	G. M., 3d cl.	Positive identification	Colon Cemetery	55	3	2	
56	Fewer, William J.	B. M., 2d cl.	Identification probable	Colon Cemetery	56	3	2	
57			Unrecognizable body	Colon Cemetery	57	3	2	
58	Holm, Gustav	B. M., 2d cl.	Identification very probable	Colon Cemetery	58	3	2	
59			Body of a large, stout man, with a long mustache, not very dark, perhaps Brofeldt	Colon Cemetery	59	3	2	
60	Eiermann, Charles F. W.	G. M., 1st cl.	Positive identification	Colon Cemetery	60	3	2	These five bodies (Nos. 60 to 64) are probably in the first grave, but not noted.
61	Jermee, Frederick	Coal-passer	Died in the San Ambrosio Hospital, Feb. 19.	Colon Cemetery	61	3		
62	Jectson, Harry	Seaman	Died in the San Ambrosio Hospital, Feb. 20.	Colon Cemetery	62	3		(The body of Jectson unaccounted for.)
63			Unrecognizable part of a body	Colon Cemetery	63	3		
64	Jenks, Carlton	G. M., 3d cl.	Identification very probable	Colon Cemetery	64	3		
65			Unrecognizable body; face blown away	Colon Cemetery	65	3		
66			Unrecognizable body	Colon Cemetery	66	3		These three bodies (Nos. 65, 66, and 67) are probably in the second grave, not noted.
67			Identification probable	Colon Cemetery	67	3		
68	Flynn, Patrick	Fireman, 2d cl.	Body short and stout, hair fairly long	Colon Cemetery	68	3	1	Lowest left.

Serial No.	Name	Rate	Character of Identification	Place of Burial	No. of Coffin	Row	Grave	Situation
69	Phillips, Francis C.	App., 1st cl.	Positive identification.	Colon Cemetery	66	7	1	Lowest right.
70	Mudd, Noble T.	Seaman	Identification probable.	Colon Cemetery	67	7		Most probably in first grave.
71	Jones, Thomas J.	Coal-passer	Positive identification.	Colon Cemetery	68	7		Lowest left.
72	McNiece, Francis J.	Coal-passer	"F. J. McN." letters on clothing.	Colon Cemetery	69	7	3	Next to lowest right.
73	Louden, James W.	App., 2d cl.	Colored boy, with "W. L." on clothing. Identification doubtful.	Colon Cemetery	70	7	3	Topmost left.
74	Lees, Samuel	Ord. Seaman	Positive identification.	Colon Cemetery	71	7	2	Lowest right.
75			Unrecognizable body.	Colon Cemetery	72	7	2	Next to lowest left.
76			Unrecognizable body.	Colon Cemetery	73	7	3	Next to lowest left.
77			Unrecognizable body.					
78	Smith, Nicholas J.	App., 1st cl.	"N" marked on part of the clothes; "Smith" on another part.	Colon Cemetery	74	7	3	Top right.
79	Simons, Alfred	Coal-passer	Identification very probable.	Colon Cemetery	75	7	2	Next to lowest right.
80			Man from 25 to 30 years, unrecognizable					
81	Conroy, Anthony	Coal-passer	Identification probable.	Colon Cemetery	76	7	2	Lowest left.
82	Barry, John P.	App., 1st cl.	Positive identification; had two rings.	Colon Cemetery	77	7	2	Next to top right.
83	Curran, Charles	Coxswain	Positive identification.	Colon Cemetery	78	7	2	Lowest left.
84			Body of a man tall and thin; "Gartrell" marked on clothing, but Gartrell saved.	Colon Cemetery	79	7	1	Next to lowest right.
85	Gordon, Joseph F.	Fireman, 1st cl.	Colored man, tall, stout, and strong, thick features and wide nostrils.	Colon Cemetery	80	4	2	Next to top left.
86		App., boy	Medium height, without mark; about 20 years.	Colon Cemetery	81	7	3	Lowest right.
87	Hughes, Patrick	Fireman, 1st cl.	Positive identification.	Colon Cemetery	82	4	2	Top right.
88	Boll, Fritz	Bayman	Body short and stout, bald about the temples, but a strip of hair on the middle of the head to the forehead. Had a knife, and $1.60 in a piece of paper.	Colon Cemetery	83	4		
89			Very small in stature, small features, mustache, age about 40 years.	Colon Cemetery	84	4	1	Lowest right.
90			Japanese, rather short and thin; no mark for recognition.	Colon Cemetery	85	4	2	Top left.
91	Donoughy, William	Ord. Seaman	Positive identification.	Colon Cemetery	86	4	3	Next to top left.
92			Young man about 25 years of age; wore ring, and had small figure of St. Joseph and package of money.	Colon Cemetery	87	4	3	Top right.
				Colon Cemetery	88	4	2	Lowest right.

Serial No.	Name	Rate	Character of Identification	Place of Burial	No. of Coffin	Row	Grave	Situation
93	Sutton, Frank	Fireman, 2d cl.	Positive identification	Colon Cemetery	89	4	3	Top left.
94	Price, Daniel	Fireman, 1st cl.	The name was found on the clothing; had $1.65 and a large knife	Colon Cemetery	90	8		These fourteen coffins (bodies No. 94 to 108) were not noted by the superintendent of the graves. They are in this row, but their situation is unknown.
95			Mutilated trunk, unrecognizable	Colon Cemetery	91	8		
96			Mutilated trunk, unrecognizable	Colon Cemetery	91	8		
97	Kniese, Frederick H.	Mach., 1st cl.	Identification very probable	Colon Cemetery	92	8		
98			Man of medium height, and very stout; had two keys	Colon Cemetery		8		
99	Gross, Henry	Landsman	Positive identification	Colon Cemetery	93	8		
100			A man about 40 years of age, stout, rather small, with a mustache, and bald at the temples	Colon Cemetery	94	8		
101	Just, Charles F.	App., 1st cl.	Positive identification	Colon Cemetery	95	8		
102	Hoyle, James	Q. M., 1st cl.	Positive identification; wore a masonic ring	Colon Cemetery	96	8		
103			Body of a boy; monogram on shirt (blue) like "I. S." combined	Colon Cemetery	97	8		
104	Johnson, George	Coal-passer	Colored, with a peculiarly shaped head and long face	Colon Cemetery	98	8		
105			Young man about 25 years of age, medium height, and stout	Colon Cemetery	99	8		
106	Horn, William J.	Fireman, 1st cl.	Identification most probable	Colon Cemetery	100	8		
107	Scully, Joseph	Boiler-maker	Identification most probable	Colon Cemetery	101	8		
108			"G. N. W." initials; coat of arms on the right arm. A man about 30 years of age, strong, and likely a fireman; had a knife	Colon Cemetery	102	8		
109	Hennekes, Albert B.	G. M., 2d cl.	Positive identification	Colon Cemetery	103	8		These two (Nos. 104 and 105) are probably in the eighth row, third grave; not noted.
110	League, James M.	Chief Yeoman	Although the initials "T. H. B." were on the arm, the body looked greatly like that of League	Colon Cemetery	104			
111	Nielsen, Sophus	Cockswain	Young man about 25 years of age, with an unfinished ship of three sails marked on the breast; coat of arms with an eagle marked on one arm; Goddess of Liberty marked on the other. Medium height and strong	Colon Cemetery	105			
112	Cole, Thomas M.	Bayman	The name "T. Codes" marked on	Colon Cemetery	106	8		Most probably in the first grave; not noted.

Serial No.	Name	Rate	Character of Identification	Place of Burial	No. of Coffin	Row	Grave	Situation
			the shirt. T. Cole is the only name we had aboard ship resembling that name. The body was a little too long for his, but the clothing was neat and the money found on him showed carefulness, and these were prominent characteristics of T. Cole. The clothing held $35	Colon Cemetery	107	3	3	Lowest right.
113..	....	....	A fireman about 35 years of age and of medium height	Colon Cemetery	108	3	3	Lowest left.
114...	Scott, Charles A........	C. M., 2d cl.	A tall boy of 18 years, with Odd Fellow links on arm	Colon Cemetery	109	3	3	Next to lowest right.
115...	....	....	Trunk of a body, unrecognizable	Colon Cemetery	110	3	3	Next to lowest left.
116...	....	....	Lower limbs of a body	Colon Cemetery	110			
117...	....	....	A man about 40 years of age, fat, and of medium height; a basket of flowers marked on the left arm, and a globe with an eagle and a flag on the right	Colon Cemetery	111	3	3	Next to top right.
118..	....	....	A body of a man between 30 and 35 years of age, tall and strong. Greatly scalded and mutilated. Had a Sacred Heart slip and 55 cents	Colon Cemetery	112	3	3	Next to top left.
119..	....	....	Body mutilated beyond recognition	Colon Cemetery	113	9		Most probably in the first grave; not noted.
120..	....	....	Trunk mutilated beyond recognition	Colon Cemetery	113			
121..	Matza, John........	Coal-passer	A man about 40 years of age; clothing marked "Mat" distinctly, and very indistinctly letters like "torza"	Colon Cemetery	114	9	1	Next to lowest right.
122..	....	....	The body of a man about 25 years of age, medium height and strong, wearing marine underclothing	Colon Cemetery	115	9		Most probably in the first grave; not noted
123..	....	....	The body of a colored man between 20 and 25 years of age, medium height and very strong. No marks on body	Colon Cemetery	116	9	1	Lowest left.

Serial No.	Name	Rate	Character of Identification	Place of Burial	No. of Coffin	Row	Grave	Situation
124	Finch, Trubie	App., boy	Positive identification	Colon Cemetery	117	9		Most probably in first grave; not noted.
125			Body of a colored man about 30 years of age, very stout, medium height; wore marine underclothing. Scalded about the neck					
126	Harry, Thomas J.	Coal-passer	Positive identification	Colon Cemetery	118	9	2	Lowest right.
127			A boy with a coat of arms on right forearm, and the Goddess of Liberty with the word "America" on the left. About 20 years of age and stout	Colon Cemetery	119	9	2	Next to lowest right.
128			A few members of an unrecognizable body	Colon Cemetery	120	9	1	Lowest right.
129	Sellers, Walter	Apothecary	Positive identification	Colon Cemetery	120	9		Most probably in second grave, top left.
130			The body of a man about 30 years old, very tall and strong. No marks on the body	Colon Cemetery	121	9		
131	Holland, Alfred J.	Cockswain	Died in San Ambrosio Hospital, Feb. 19	Colon Cemetery	122	9	1	Next to lowest left.
132			The body of a man about 40 years of age, medium height and very strong; on the right arm, a star of five points; on the left, the head of a woman with a sailor's cap, and a flag	Colon Cemetery	123	9	2	Next to top right.
133	Tigges, Frank B.	Coppersmith	The body of a German; breast marked with an eagle, and over it "Von Fels zum Mieis"; on the left forearm, a mermaid. The man was about 30 years of age, quite tall, and strong	Colon Cemetery	124	9	3	Lowest right.
134			Boy about 25 years of age, medium height and fairly strong; clothes marked like "Burghard." A skeleton key found on the body	Colon Cemetery	125	9		Most probably the coffin next to lowest right, in the third grave.
135	Burkhardt, Robert	Q. M., 2d cl.	Paper found in the pocket with the name Burkhardt. The body of a man about 25 years of age, medium height and strong; money in the clothing	Colon Cemetery	126	9	3	Lowest left.
				Colon Cemetery	127	9	2	Lowest left.

Serial No.	Name	Rate	Character of Identification	Place of Burial	No. of Coffin	Row	Grave	Situation
136	Fisher, Frank	Ord. Seaman	Died on the Spanish steamer Colon, Feb. 20	Colon Cemetery	128	9	2	Next to lowest left.
137			Unrecognizable trunk of a body	Colon Cemetery	129	9	3	Next to top left.
138			Fireman about 35 years of age, medium height, strong and fat; no marks on the body. Blue underclothing. Scalded on front of body					
139			Japanese about 25 years of age, medium height and strong. Flannel undershirt and linen drawers. Hair appeared to be red.	Colon Cemetery	130	9		Most probably in the third grave; not noted.
140			The body of a man about 30 years of age, strong, fat, and short. On the right forearm a peculiar mark of gray and red, likely two stars partly overlapping each other; under the left forearm, pictures of a man and a woman with clasped hands,—the woman's neck adorned with a necklace and a locket,—and beneath the clasped hands, a heart	Colon Cemetery	131	9		Most probably in the third grave; not noted.
141	Harris, Millard F.	Q. M., 3d cl.	A colored man, very large; dressed in seaman's trousers, shirt, and jersey. This name was found on a handkerchief found in a pocket.	Colon Cemetery	132	9	3	Next to lowest left.
142			The members of a large man. In a pocket of the clothes were two keys attached to a piece of brass on which was written "Patrick O'Hara, Albany St., Roxbury, Mass."; also was found in the clothes a key without a loop. No mark on person or clothes. Underclothing of cambric	Colon Cemetery	133	9		Most probably in the first grave; not noted.
143			The body of a colored man about 40 years, very tall and stout. On the left arm the picture of a Goddess of Liberty with wings, and	Colon Cemetery	134	9		Most probably these two bodies (Nos. 142 and 143) are in the first grave; not noted.

Serial No.	Name	Rate	Character of Identification	Place of Burial	No. of Coffin	Row	Grave	Situation
144	....	....	under it the words, "Young America", on the right arm, Odd Fellow links, and under them "Hold fast", above these links a heart pierced with a knife .... Japanese about 35 years of age, medium height and very stout. $40 were found on the body. No marks on the body. It was found near the conning-tower.	Colon Cemetery	135	9		Most probably in first grave; not noted.
145	Lund, William	Coxswain	The body of a man about 30 years of age, medium height, with a light mustache. No marks on the body. $40 were found on the body. The name "Lund" on the clothing.	Colon Cemetery	136	9		
146	Bennet, J	Marine	Limbs of a man, stout and medium height; marine underclothing, on which were the initials "J. B.".	Colon Cemetery	137	8	3	Next to top right.
147	....	....	Probably a Japanese about 30 years of age; blue underclothing marked "N. T. M." On the back of the left hand, between the forefinger and thumb, the picture of an anchor; and on the left forearm, an anchor with sun-rays over it; on the left muscle an eagle. Some marks also were on the right arm and muscle and on the breast, but they could not be discerned. On a piece of paper the address, "Miss Susan Jones, 55 Williamson Lane, Norfolk, Va." The name "N. T. Mix" or "Mudd" was also on the clothing. On a letter-head was printed "St. Mark's Hotel, Fifth Avenue and 39th Street, New York," and on another letter the address, "2627 West 47th Street," without a name	Colon Cemetery	138	9		Most likely in first grave; not noted.
				Colon Cemetery	139	8	2	Lowest right.

Serial No.	Name	Rate	Character of Identification	Place of Burial	No. of Coffin	Row	Grave	Situation
148	Koebler, George W	App., 1st cl.	Died in San Ambrosio Hospital, Feb. 22	Colon Cemetery	140	3	2	Next to top left.
149			Nos. 149 to 156 were the charred remains of these eight bodies, principally ashes					
150				Colon Cemetery	141	7	2	Next to lowest left. The remains of these eight bodies (Nos. 149 to 156) are buried in one coffin.
151				Colon Cemetery	141	7	2	
152				Colon Cemetery	141	7	2	
153				Colon Cemetery	141	7	2	
154				Colon Cemetery	141	7	2	
155				Colon Cemetery	141	7	2	
156				Colon Cemetery	141	7	2	
157			Trunk and two arms. No marks	Colon Cemetery	142	7	2	Top right.
158			The body of a man about 40 years of age, tall and strong	Colon Cemetery	142	7	2	Next to top right.
159			The body of a young man about 18 years of age, medium height, quite strong, and average weight. The body had marine underclothing, and was found at the hatch forward of the marine compartment	Colon Cemetery	143	7	2	
160			Charred head and trunk	Colon Cemetery	144	8	2	Lowest left.
161			The body of a fireman about 40 years of age, tall and strong, with no marks on the body. The lower teeth were very uneven	Colon Cemetery	145	8	2	Next to lowest right.
162			The body of a man about 45 years of age, dressed in marine underclothing. Likely an oiler or machinist. Oil soaked in the underclothing	Colon Cemetery	146	8	3	Lowest right.
163			The body of a white man about five feet nine inches in height, and 45 years of age; fairly stout and strong; marine underclothing. No marks on the body or the clothing	Colon Cemetery	147	8	3	Lowest left.
164	Johnson, J. W.	Landsman	Young man about 25 years of age,	Colon Cemetery	148	8	3	Next to lowest right.

Serial No.	Name	Rate	Character of Identification	Place of Burial	No. of Coffin	Row	Grave	Situation
165	Holzer, Frederick C.	Ord. Seaman	very tall and strong; mark of "K" or "X" on shoulders. "J. W. Johnson" marked on drawers	Colon Cemetery	149	8	3	Next to top left.
166			Died in San Ambrosio Hospital, Feb. 25	Colon Cemetery	150	6	1	Alone in this grave.
167			Young man; white; an eagle worked on the right arm, and under the eagle flags whose stars are immediately under the wings of the eagle	Colon Cemetery	151	8	3	Top right.
168			Young man between 20 and 25 years of age; quite strong; about five feet eight inches in height; with marine underclothing	Key West	{152 B.*1			
			Man about 35 years of age, medium height; no mark on the body	Key West	{153 B.2			
169 170	White, Robert	Mess-attendant	Only part of the trunk and the arms. Colored man; clothing marked "K. E. Y. K. E. R. Dg.," and again, "A. W." or "M." In a pocket were found two storage-room keys and wine-locker keys of the ward-room	Key West	{154 B.3			These two (Nos. 169 and 170) in one coffin or box.
171	Pinkney, James	Mess-attendant	Only a few pieces of bones with a blue coat having pockets and black buttons. The letter "R" on a handkerchief	Key West	{154 B.3			
172			White man about 25 or 30 years of age, medium height and very strong; marine underclothing well soaked with oil; probably an oiler or machinist	Key West	{155 B.4			
173	Wagner, Henry	1st Ser. Marines	A man about 40 years of age, exceedingly tall and well built; long features; marine underclothing	Key West	{156 B.5			
174			Body of a white man about 35 years of age; medium height; very fine underclothing of blue. The letters	Key West	{157 B.6			

* Box.

Serial No.	Name	Rate	Character of Identification	Place of Burial	No. of Coffin	Row	Grave	Situation
175	....	....	"He" on the clothing; the next letter like "h" or "n." Perhaps Herriman or Carr. The body seems too stout for the former, but this is the only body unaccounted for in "He." It may be he gave his shirt to Carr or Keiger, who were on the dynamo force...... Only head and upper body, unrecognizable	Key West......	{ 158 { B. 7			
176	....	....	Only trunk and lower limbs; sailor's outer trousers; 25 cents in one pocket	Key West......	{ 159 { B. 8			
177	....	....	A man about 40 years of age, medium height. On right forearm, a mark like two hearts overlapping each other, with two daggers piercing them from the upper part; above them a mark like a leaf; the whole in blue, except a tinge of red in the leaf. Under-shirt was of blue. No name on the clothing.	Key West......	{ 160 { B. 9			
178	Schoen, Joseph,........ or Suman, E. B.	Cor. of Marines Private Mar.	Body of a young man about 25 years of age, medium height and strong. Body was of a white man, with no marks. Marine underclothing.	Key West......	{ 161 { B. 10			
179	Lieut. Friend W. Jenkins	Lieut. (J. G.)	Positive identification	Key West......	{ 162 { B. 11			
180	Rushworth, William......	Ch. Mach	A mark on the left forearm like an anchor, but only top of it was discernible owing to the decay of the arm. Clothing blue and very good. Body of a man rather tall, five feet eight or nine inches, and rather stout, and about 45 years of age. Many keys found in the pockets, and a bill-head: "Cabelleros Hovenes y Muchachos. Baules y Saccos. De los Callos Duval y	Allegheny Cem., Pittsburg, Pa.	{ 163 { B. 12			

Serial No.	Name	Rate	Character of Identification	Place of Burial	No. of Coffin	Row	Grave	Situation
181	Suzuki, Kashotora	Mess-attendant	Wall No. 400. Also No. 700 Duval St., Fla.	Key West	164 / B. 13			
182			Japanese, very small, quite stout, about 25 years of age; blue shirt; no marks on body or clothing	Key West	165 / B. 14			
183			Young man about 25 or 30 years of age, great height, very strong; white man about six feet tall. Underclothing was blue. No marks on clothing or body. It came up from forward part of the ship	Key West	166 / B. 15			
184			A very tall man, about six feet tall; underclothing of blue; no marks on clothing or body. The body was of a man about 40 years of age. It came from the forward part of the ship	Key West	167 / B. 16			
185			Young man about 25 years of age. Small head like that of a Japanese, but rather too tall and stout for such. Medium height and very strong. Undershirt blue, drawers white (marine). No mark on clothing or body. The body came from the after-part of the ship	Key West	168 / B. 17			
			Initials "A. Z," found on underclothing, which was marine. The body of a man about 35 or 40 years of age, very tall and strong. The body came from the middle or forward part of the ship	Key West	169 / B. 18			
186			Boy about 18 years of age, white, small, about five feet two or three inches tall; marine underclothing, no mark on clothing or body. It came up from the forward part of the ship	Key West	170 / B. 19			

Serial No.	Name	Rate	Character of Identification	Place of Burial	No. of Coffin	Row	Grave	Situation
187			Body of a man about 42 years of age; very tall, about six feet; very strong; fully dressed, with pointed shoes, but no mark on the clothing. Found in the ten-inch loading-room	Key West	171 B. 20			

ADDITIONS BY CAPTAIN C. D. SIGSBEE, U. S. N., FROM THE RECORDS OF THE NAVY DEPARTMENT

Serial No.	Name	Rate	Character of Identification	Place of Burial	No. of Coffin	Row	Grave	Situation
	Anderson, John	B. M., 2d cl.	Identified	Key West				
	Andrews, Frank	Ord. Seaman	Identified	Key West				
			Unrecognized body	Key West				
			Unrecognized body	Key West				
			Unrecognized body	Key West				

This shows a total of one hundred and ninety-two bodies buried in one hundred and seventy-six coffins.

C. D. S.

www.ingramcontent.com/pod-product-compliance
Lightning Source LLC
Chambersburg PA
CBHW030406230426
43664CB00007BB/775